October 4-7, 2017
Rochester, NY, USA

Association for Computing Machinery

Advancing Computing as a Science & Profession

RIIT'17

Proceedings of the 6th Annual Conference on
Research in Information Technology

Sponsored by:

ACM SIGITE

Supported by:

Dell EMC, Oracle Academy, TuringsCraft, Illinois Institute of Technology, Rochester Institute of Technology, & Wentworth Institute of Technology

**Association for
Computing Machinery**

Advancing Computing as a Science & Profession

The Association for Computing Machinery
2 Penn Plaza, Suite 701
New York, New York 10121-0701

Notice to Past Authors of ACM-Published Articles

ISBN: 978-1-4503-5120-1 (Digital)

ISBN: 978-1-4503-5606-0 (Print)

Additional copies may be ordered prepaid from:

ACM Order Department
PO Box 30777
New York, NY 10087-0777, USA

Phone: 1-800-342-6626 (USA and Canada)
+1-212-626-0500 (Global)
Fax: +1-212-944-1318
E-mail: acmhelp@acm.org
Hours of Operation: 8:30 am – 4:30 pm ET

SIGITE 2017 Conference Chair's Welcome

It is with great pleasure that I welcome you to Rochester, NY, site of the 18th Annual Conference on Information Technology Education (SIGITE 2017) and the 6th Annual Conference on Research in Information Technology (RIIT 2017). The Information Sciences and Technologies Department of Rochester Institute of Technology is proud to once again serve as the host for this premier set of conferences. Our Program Chairs, Tom Ayers and Dan Bogaard, have put together a great program, and I thank them for all of their work putting the program together. I also want to thank our Sponsorship Chairs, Bryan Goda and Hollis Greenburg for their work as well. And certainly, a huge thank you to the sponsors themselves.

The BS Information Technology program at RIT, established in 1991, was one of the very first IT programs in the country. Thursday evening you'll be able to have a tour of the facilities—I hope you take advantage of it. Our dinner Thursday evening will also feature a selection of local Rochester foods—you'll get to try red and white hots, the famous Garbage Plate, and many other unique foods. I also hope you have time to visit Rochester while you are here. In addition to the George Eastman Museum, the Strong Museum of Play, and many other special venues, we are home to many craft breweries and close by to New York's wine region. You can sample some of these by taking part in our excursions on Wednesday evening and Saturday afternoon.

The conference will be at the Hyatt Regency in downtown Rochester, not far from the Genesee River and the waterfalls that were responsible for Rochester's early claim to fame as a milling town and its original moniker, "Flour City". Today Rochester is known as the "Flower City" with numerous parks throughout the city featuring many species of flowers, but none as famous as the Highland Park lilacs that are featured every May. In addition to touring the Upper Falls and the parks, you can also visit nearby museums and other dedications commemorating the work of abolitionists and activists such as Frederick Douglas and Susan B. Anthony.

I hope you enjoy the conference and get to know Rochester during your stay. Please, let me know if you have any questions.

Steve Zilora
SIGITE/RIIT 2017 Conference Chair
Rochester Institute of Technology, USA

Program Chairs' Welcome

It is our great pleasure to welcome you to the 18th Annual Conference on Information Technology Education (SIGITE 2017) and the 6th Annual Conference on Research in Information Technology (RIIT 2017). The theme this year is "Enabling the Future", with a focus on the need for preparing Information Technology students for a future that includes defining the Internet of Things (IoT). Rochester is a fitting place for this theme, as it has long been a city that has leveraged the technological innovations of the day. The Erie Canal allowed Rochester millers to ship their flour across the state to Albany (earning it the nickname, "Flour City"), and flexible photographic film allowed George Eastman to grow his Kodak empire. The canal, and the flexible film are enablers, but with the Internet of Things, ubiquitous computing, and smart communities; information technology is the enabler.

This year, 90 reviewers conducted a total of 384 reviews of 94 submissions of papers, panels, posters, lightning talks, and workshops. For RIIT, 6 of 11 papers were accepted for a 54% acceptance rate; for SIGITE, 23 of 58 papers were accepted for a 39% acceptance rate. A great deal of thanks goes to both the reviewers and, of course, the authors for their excellent work. Not surprisingly, both RIIT and SIGITE papers have a preponderance of topics such as IoT, ubiquitous computing, and dealing with interconnectivity. While many of the papers relate to this year's theme, you will also find papers on curriculum development, capstone ideas, and innovative lab and classroom approaches among a variety of other IT education topics.

SIGITE/RIIT 2017 runs from Thursday to Saturday and is preceded by the annual Chairs and Program Directors Meeting, and vendor workshops on Thursday morning. The formal program begins on Thursday at noon. The program offers a combination of papers, and lightning talks on research in progress, and concludes with a dinner reception for networking with colleagues old and new. Friday features additional paper sessions and lightning talks for SIGITE and RIIT, a poster session in the afternoon, and concludes with a reception for Community College educators. Those not attending the community college reception can find dinner at one of the many nearby restaurants. On Saturday morning, the conference continues with additional papers and an author-submitted workshop. The conference concludes Saturday at 11a.m. Rochester, friends, and lots of opportunities to share—all the necessary ingredients for a great experience. We hope to see you at SIGITE/RIIT 2017 where we can not only discuss "Enabling Our Future", but we can also build new alliances for the future. Thank you!

Dan Bogaard
SIGITE/RIIT 2017 Program Co-Chair
Rochester Institute of Technology, Rochester NY, USA

Tom Ayers
SIGITE/RIIT 2017 Program Co-Chair
Broward College, Fort Lauderdale FL, USA

Table of Contents

RIIT 2017 Conference

Conference Chair: Stephen Zilora *(Rochester Institute of Technology, USA)*

Program Chairs: Thomas Ayers *(Broward College, USA)*
Daniel Bogaard *(Rochester Institute of Technology, USA)*

Sponsorship Chairs: Bryan Goda *(University of Washington Tacoma, USA)*
Hollis Greenburg *(Wentworth Institute of Technology, USA)*

Reviewers: Shereef Abu Al-Maati *(American University of Kuwait, Kuwait)*
Vangel Ajanovski *(Saints Cyril and Methodius University, Macedonia)*
Zahra Alqubaiti *(Kennesaw State University, USA)*
Frank Appunn *(Northcentral University, USA)*
Victor Arenas *(Broward College, USA)*
William Armitage *(University of South Florida, USA)*
Prateek Basavaraj *(University of Central Florida, USA)*
Angela Berardinelli *(Mercyhurst University, USA)*
Larry Booth *(Clayton State University, USA)*
Reinhardt Botha *(Nelson Mandela Metropolitan University, South Africa)*
Redjem Bouhenguel *(Broward College, USA)*
Yu Cai *(Michigan Technological University, USA)*
Brian Canada *(University of South Carolina Beaufort, USA)*
Ankur Chattopadhyay *(University of Wisconsin Green Bay, USA)*
Sam Chung *(Southern Illinois University, USA)*
Bill Dafnis *(Capella University, USA)*
Joan E. DeBello *(St. John's University, USA)*
Maxime Descos *(Illinois Institute of Technology, USA)*
Ronald Erdei *(University of South Carolina Beaufort, USA)*
Stephanie Etter *(Broward College, USA)*
Pedro Guillermo Feijóo García *(Universidad El Bosque, Columbia)*
Alan Flaten *(Broward College, USA)*
Bryan French *(Rochester Institute of Technology, USA)*
Rob Friedman *(Montclair State University, USA)*
Ilenia Fronza *(Free University of Bolzano, Italy)*
Chunming Gao *(University of Washington Tacoma, USA)*
Sandra Gorka *(Pennsylvania College of Technology, USA)*
Hollis Greenberg *(Wentworth Institute of Technology, USA)*
Meng Han *(Kennesaw State University, USA)*
Eiji Hayashiguchi *(Informatiom Technology Promotion Agency, Japan)*
Richard Helps *(Brigham Young University, USA)*
Larry Hill *(Rochester Institute of Technology, USA)*
Edward Holden *(Rochester Institute of Technology, USA)*
Rick Homkes *(Purdue University, USA)*

RIIT 2017 Sponsor & Supporters

Sponsor:

Supporters:

Identifying Grey Sheep Users By The Distribution of User Similarities In Collaborative Filtering

Yong Zheng
School of Applied Technology
Illinois Institute of Technology
Chicago, Illinois, USA 60616
yzheng66@iit.edu

Mayur Agnani
School of Applied Technology
Illinois Institute of Technology
Chicago, Illinois, USA 60616
magnani@hawk.iit.edu

Mili Singh
School of Applied Technology
Illinois Institute of Technology
Chicago, Illinois, USA 60616
msingh32@hawk.iit.edu

ABSTRACT

Recommender Systems have been successfully applied to alleviate the information overload problem and assist the process of decision making. Collaborative filtering, as one of the most popular recommendation algorithms, has been fully explored and developed in the past two decades. However, one of the challenges in collaborative filtering, the problem of "Grey Sheep" user, is still under investigation. "Grey Sheep" users is a group of the users who have special tastes and they may neither agree nor disagree with the majority of the users. The identification of them becomes a challenge in collaborative filtering, since they may introduce difficulties to produce accurate collaborative recommendations. In this paper, we propose a novel approach which can identify the Grey Sheep users by reusing the outlier detection techniques based on the distribution of user-user similarities. Our experimental results based on the MovieLens 10M rating data demonstrate the ease and effectiveness of our proposed approach.

CCS CONCEPTS

• **Information systems** → **Recommender systems**;

KEYWORDS

recommender system; collaborative filtering; grey sheep

1 INTRODUCTION

Recommender system is one of the information systems which assist user's decision making by recommending a list of appropriate items to the end users tailored to their preferences. It has been successfully applied to a number of applications, such as e-commerce (e.g., Amazon, eBay), online streaming (e.g., Netflix, Pandora), social networks (e.g., Facebook, Twitter), tourism (e.g., Tripadvisor) and restaurant (e.g., Yelp), etc.

Several recommender systems have been developed to provide accurate item recommendations. There are three types of these algorithms: collaborative filtering approaches, content-based recommendation algorithms and the hybrid recommendation models [3]. Collaborative filtering (CF) is one of the most popular algorithms

since it is effective and it does not rely on any content information. CF is also cost-inexpensive and easy to be interpreted. It has been well developed and applied in real practice, such as the recommendation applications on Amazon.com.

Most of the efforts by the research communities were made to improve the effectiveness of the CF algorithms, while far too little attention has been paid to the problem of "Grey Sheep" users which is one of the challenges in collaborative filtering. J. McCrae, et al. categorize the users into three classes [10]: "the majority of the users fall into the class of *White Sheep* users, where these users have high rating correlations with several other users. The *Black Sheep* users usually have very few or even no correlating users, and the case of black sheep users is an acceptable failure [1]. The bigger problem exists in the group of *Grey Sheep* users, where these users have different opinions or unusual tastes which result in low correlations with many users; and they also cause odd recommendations for their correlated users". Therefore, Grey Sheep (GS) user usually refers to "a small number of individuals who would not benefit from pure collaborative filtering systems because their opinions do not consistently agree or disagree with any group of people [5]".

Related research point out that GS users must be identified from the data and treated individually for these reasons:

- They may leave negative impact on the quality of recommendations for the White Sheep users [5–8, 10, 12, 13], especially when it comes to the collaborative filtering algorithms
- Collaborative filtering approaches do not work well for GS users [5–8, 12]. GS users should be treated separately with another type of the recommendation models, such as content-based approaches, even if there are limited number of GS users in the data.
- Due to the presence of GS users, the poor recommendations may result in critical consequences [5, 8, 10]: unsatisfied users, user defection, failure among learners, inaccurate marketing or advertising strategies, etc

There are two significant characteristics of GS users indicated by the related research: On one hand, *GS users do not agree or disagree with other users* [6, 10]. Researchers believe GS users may fall on the boundary of the user groups. Ghazanfar, et al. [6, 7] introduces a clustering technique to identify the GS users, while Gras, et al. [8] reuses the outlier detection based on the user's rating distributions. On the other hand, *GS users may have low correlations with many other users, and they have very few highly correlated*

RIIT'17, October 4–7, 2017, Rochester, NY, USA.
© 2017 ACM. ISBN 978-1-4503-5120-1/17/10…$15.00
DOI: https://doi.org/10.1145/3125649.3125651

---

[1]The problem of black sheep users is caused by the situation that we do not have rich or even no rating profiles for these users. It is acceptable failure since the problem can be alleviated or solved if these users will continue to leave more ratings on the items.

neighbors [5]. Unfortunately, no previous study has investigated how to take advantage of this characteristics to identify GS users in the recommender systems.

In this paper, we make the first attempt to identify GS users by exploring the distribution of user similarities or correlations. More specifically, we statistically analyze a user's correlations with all of the other users, figure out bad and good examples, and reuse the outlier detections to identify potential GS users. Statistical test is applied to examine whether the recommendation performance by the collaborative filtering approach is significantly worse for these identified GS users and other common users. The proposed approach is evaluated based on the popular MovieLens rating data.

2 RELATED WORK

We introduce collaborative filtering first, and discuss corresponding progress of GS user identification in this section.

2.1 Preliminary: Collaborative Filtering

Recommender systems have been demonstrated as useful tools to assist user's decision making. For example, Netflix may recommend a list of movies that you may be interested in, and Amazon may suggest appropriate books that you may want to purchase, while users do not need to issue a query to look for something they want. The idea behind these recommender systems is that the recommendation model can infer which items a user may like based on user's preference history, such as how a user rates a movie, which items they browse online, or the purchase/order history in user profiles.

Table 1: Example of a Movie Rating Data

	Pirates of the Caribbean 4	Kung Fu Panda 2	Harry Potter 6	Harry Potter 7
U_1	4	4	1	2
U_2	3	4	2	1
U_3	2	2	4	4
U_4	4	4	1	?

Rating prediction is a common task in the recommender systems. Take the movie rating data shown in Table 1 for example, there are four users and four movies. The values in the data matrix represent users' rating on corresponding movies. We have the knowledge about how the four users rate these movies. And we'd like to learn from the knowledge and predict how the user U_4 will rate the movie "Harry Potter 7".

One of the most popular recommendation algorithms is collaborative filtering [10, 13]. There are memory-based collaborative filtering, such as the user-based collaborative filtering (UBCF) [11], and model-based collaborative filtering, such as matrix factorization. In this paper, we focus on the UBCF since it may suffer from the problem of GS users seriously.

The assumption in UBCF is that a user's rating on one movie is similar to the preferences on the same movie by a group of K users. This group of the users is well known as K nearest neighbors (KNN). Namely, they are the top-K users who have similar tastes with a given user. Take Table 1 for example, to find the KNN for user U_4, we observe the ratings given by the four users on the given movies except "Harry Potter 7". We can see that U_1 and U_2 actually give similar ratings as U_4 – high ratings (3 or 4-star) on the first two

movies and low rating on the movie "Harry Potter 6". Therefore, we infer that U_4 may rate the movie "Harry Potter 7" similarly as how the U_1 and U_2 rate the same movie.

To identify the KNN, we can use similarity measures to calculate user-user similarities or correlations, such as the cosine similarity shown by Equation 1.

$$sim(U_i, U_j) = \frac{\overrightarrow{R_{U_i}} \bullet \overrightarrow{R_{U_j}}}{\|\overrightarrow{R_{U_i}}\|_2 \times \|\overrightarrow{R_{U_j}}\|_2} \qquad (1)$$

We use a rating matrix similar to Table 1 to represent our data. $\overrightarrow{R_{U_i}}$ and $\overrightarrow{R_{U_j}}$ are the row vectors for user U_i and U_j respectively, where the rating is set as zero if a user did not rate the item. The size of these rating vectors is the same as the number of movies. In Equation 1, the numerator represents the dot product of the two user vectors, while the denominator is the multiplication of two Euclidean norms (i.e, L2 norms). The value of K in KNN refers to the number of the top similar neighbors we need in the rating prediction functions. We need to tune up the performance by varying different numbers for K.

Once the KNN are identified, we can predict how a user rates one item by the rating function described by Equation 2.

$$P_{a,t} = \bar{r}_a + \frac{\sum\limits_{u \in N} (r_{u,t} - \bar{r}_u) \times sim(a, u)}{\sum\limits_{u \in N} sim(a, u)} \qquad (2)$$

where $P_{a,t}$ represents the predicted rating for user a on the item t. N is the top-K nearest neighborhood of users a, and u is one of the users in this neighborhood. The *sim* function is a similarity measure to calculate user-user similarities or correlations, while we use cosine similarity in our experiments. Accordingly, $r_{u,t}$ is neighbor u's rating on item t, $\bar{r}_a$ is user a's average rating over all items, and $\bar{r}_u$ is u's average rating.

This prediction function tries to aggregate KNN's ratings on the item t to estimate how user a rates t. However, the predicted ratings may be not accurate if user a is a GS user, since the user similarities or correlations between a and his or her neighbors may be very low. From another perspective, if a GS user is selected as one of the neighbors for a common user, it may result in odd recommendations or predictions since GS users may have unusual tastes on the items.

2.2 Grey Sheep User Identifications

There are several research [5, 10, 12, 13] that point out the problem of GS user, define or summarize the characteristics of GS users, but very few of the existing work were made to figure out the solutions to identify GS users.

As mentioned previously, there are two mainstream statements as the characteristics for the GS users: *GS users do not agree or disagree with other users* [6, 10]. Researchers believe GS users may fall on the boundary of the user groups. Ghazanfar, et al. [6, 7] proposes a clustering technique to identify the GS users, while they define improved centroid selection methods and isolates the GS users from the user community by setting different user similarity thresholds. The main drawback in their approach is the difficulty to find the optimal number of clusters, as well as the high computation cost to end up convergence in the clustering process, not to mention the unpredictable varieties by initial settings and other parameters in the technique. In their experiments, they demonstrate that content-based recommendation algorithms can be applied to improve the recommendation performance for the GS users. By contrast, Gras, et al. [8] reuses the outlier detection based on the user's rating distributions. They additionally take the imprecision of ratings (i.e., prediction errors) into account. However, the rating prediction error can only be used to evaluate whether a user is a GS user, it may not be appropriate to utilize it to identify GS users. It is because GS user is not the only reason that leads to large prediction errors. From another perspective, a user associated with large prediction errors is not necessary to be a GS user.

Another characteristics is that *GS users may have low correlations with many other users, and they have very few highly correlated neighbors* [5]. Unfortunately, no previous study has investigated how to take advantage of this characteristics to identify GS users in the recommender systems. This characteristics is highly related to the distribution of user-user similarities or correlations. In this paper, we make the first attempt to identify GS users by exploring the distribution of their user correlations. Note that our work is different from the Gras, et al. [8]'s work, since they stay to work on the distribution of user ratings, while we exploit the distribution of user similarities.

3 METHODOLOGIES

As mentioned in [5], White Sheep users are the common users that have high correlations with other users. Namely, we can find a set of good KNN for White Sheep users. By contrast, GS users have correlations with other users but most of the correlations are relatively low.

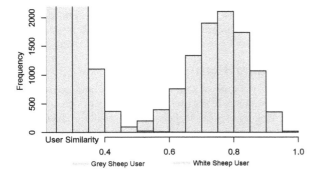

Figure 1: Distribution of User Similarities by Example of White Sheep and Grey Sheep Users

For each user, we are able to obtain his or her similarities with other users based on the cosine similarity described by Equation 1. The distribution of user similarities can be depicted by a histogram as shown in Figure 1. The x-axis is the value of user similarities, and the y-axis tells how many similarities values (i.e., the frequency) fall in each bin of the user similarities. A White Sheep user usually has higher correlations with other users, therefore its distribution of user similarities is expected to be left-skewed and the frequency at higher similarities should be significantly larger. In terms of

the GS users, we do not have many high correlations with other users, and most of the user similarities are low. It may result in the blue histogram in Figure 1 which presents a heavily right-skewed distribution.

Imagine that there could be thousands of or even more users in a data set. The process of identifying the GS users becomes the procedure of distinguishing GS users from the White Sheep users, where the distribution of user similarities for GS users may meet the following requirements:

- It is usually a right-skewed distribution.
- The descriptive statistics of the user similarities, such as the first, second and third quartiles (q1, q2, q3), as well as the mean of the correlations, may be relatively smaller, since GS users have low correlations with other users.

However, it is difficult to define how small the user similarity is we can say the user is a GS user. The same thing happens to the degree of the skewness. It may not be practical to simply define a threshold for the user similarities or the skewness of the distributions to identify the GS users.

Outlier detection [4, 9], as a result, becomes one of the potential solutions to help us distinguish GS users from the group of common users. It refers to the process of the identification of observations which do not conform to an expected pattern or other items in a dataset [4]. The idea behind is that we can detect abnormal observations by defining the common or good examples in the data. The outlier detection could be a supervised, unsupervised or semi-supervised learning process. Gras, et al. [8]'s work also points out that the identification of GS users is closely related to the outlier detection problem in data mining.

Our proposed methodologies can be summarized by the following four steps: distribution representations, example selection, outlier detection and examination of GS users.

3.1 Distribution Representations

The first step is to obtain user-user similarities and represent the distribution of user similarities for each user in the data set. We use the cosine similarity described by Equation 1 to calculate the user-user similarity between every pair of the users. Note that the similarity of two users may be zero if there are no co-rated items by them. We remove the zero similarities from the distribution, since we only focus on the known user-user similarities in our data.

Table 2: Example of Distribution Representations

User	q1	q2	q3	Mean	STD	Skewness
40459	0.051	0.089	0.133	0.098	0.060	0.964
7266	0.028	0.056	0.091	0.064	0.045	1.245
34975	0.128	0.181	0.243	0.193	0.093	0.671
34974	0.093	0.149	0.209	0.156	0.084	0.568
34977	0.047	0.077	0.121	0.112	0.115	2.516
...	...	...	...	...	...	...

As a result, we are able to obtain a list of non-zero user-user similarities for each user. We further represent each user by the descriptive statistics of his or her distribution of the user similarities, including, q1, q2, q3, mean, standard deviation (STD) and skewness, as shown by Table 2.

3.2 Example Selection

To apply the outlier detection, we need to select *good* (i.e., White Sheep users) and *bad* (i.e., potential GS users) examples in order to construct a user matrix similar to Table 2. This step is necessary especially when there are large scale of the users in the matrix. Note that we are not going to label these examples, since we are not exactly sure which users are White Sheep or GS users, and the following outlier detection technique we use is not a supervised learning process.

According to the definition of White Sheep and GS users in [5], we can find many highly correlated neighbors with White Sheep users, while GS users usually have relatively low correlations with others. We believe the good examples may have higher values in similarity statistics, including the q1, q2, q3 and mean similarity in Table 2. By contrast, these statistics for bad examples may be much lower. In addition, the distribution of user similarities associated with the good examples may be left-skewed, while it is more likely to be right-skewed for the bad examples, as shown in Figure 1.

We suggest to filter the users by the descriptive statistics of their similarity distributions, such as the first quartile (q1), the second quartile (q2), the third quartile (q3), as well as mean of the similarity values, etc. More specifically, the bad examples could be selected by the following constraints:

- **Low similarity statistics**: In this case, q1, q2, q3 and mean may be much smaller than other users. We can select a lower-bound as the threshold. For example, if a user's mean similarity is smaller than *the first quartile* of mean similarities (i.e., the list of mean values over all of the users), this user is selected as one of the bad examples. The constraints could be flexible. They can be applied to the mean similarity only, or they could be applied to any subsets of {q1, q2, q3, mean} at the same time.
- **The degree of skewness**: This time, we apply a constraint on the skewness. For example, if a user's skewness value in his or her similarity distribution is larger than *the third quartile* of skewness values over all of the users, this user may be selected as one of the bad examples. It is because GS users may have very few highly correlated neighbors, and most of their user correlations are pretty low, which results in a heavily right-skewed similarity distribution.

Again, the constraints could be very flexible. On one hand, they can be applied on any selected descriptive statistics, such as q1, mean or skewness. On another hand, the threshold could be any reasonable ones. For example, we can set the threshold as *the first quartile* of mean similarities or the *average value* of mean similarities. Flexible constraints may select large proportion of the bad examples, while the strict constraints may result in limited number of candidates. The best selection may vary from data to data. We use similar strategy to select the good examples, but the good examples must have high similarity statistics and a relatively left-skewed distribution of the user similarities.

3.3 Outlier Detection

There are several outlier detection [4, 9] techniques, such as the probabilistic likelihood approach, the clustering based or the density based methods, etc. In this paper, we adopt a density based

method which relies on the local outlier factor (LOF) [2]. LOF is based on the notion of local density, where locality is given by the k nearest neighbors[2] whose distance is used to estimate the density. The nearest neighbor, in our case, can be produced by using distance metrics on the feature matrix, while the feature matrix is the distribution representation matrix as shown in Table 2. By comparing the local density of a user to the local densities of his or her neighbors, one can identify regions of similar density, and the users that have a substantially lower density than their neighbors can be viewed as the outliers (i.e., the GS users) finally. Due to that the distances among the users are required to be calculated, we apply a normalization to the matrix in Table 2 in order to make sure all of the columns are in the same scale.

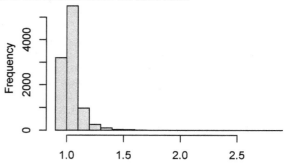

Figure 2: Histogram of LOF Scores

Figure 2 presents an example of the histogram of LOF scores, while x-axis represents the LOF score and each score is associated with a single user. A user will be viewed as a common user if his or her LOF score is close to the value of 1.0. By contrast, it can be an outlier (i.e., GS user) if the LOF score is significantly larger or smaller than 1.0. We set a threshold for the LOF score, and tune up the results by varying the values of k and the LOF threshold in our experiments in order to find qualified GS users as many as possible.

3.4 Examinations

With different values of k and the LOF threshold, we are able to collect different sets of the users as the outliers or GS users. We use the following approaches to examine the quality of the GS users:

- The recommendation performance for the group of GS users by collaborative filtering must be significantly worse than the performance for the White Sheep users. More specifically, the average rating prediction errors (see Section 4.1) based on the rating profiles associated with these GS users must be significantly higher than the errors that are associated with non-GS users. If the prediction errors for GS users and the remaining group of the users are close, we will perform two-independent sample statistical test to examine the degree of significance.
- We additionally visualize the distribution of similarities for GS users, in comparison with the one by non-GS users. The ideal visualization is expected to be similar to the one shown by Figure 1, where the distributions for GS and White sheep users are right and left-skewed respectively.

---

[2]We use k to distinguish it from the K in KNN based UBCF algorithm.

By meeting the basic requirements above, we continue to tune up the values of k and the LOF threshold, in order to find GS users as many as possible. But note that GS users are always a small proportion of the users in the data.

4 EXPERIMENTS AND RESULTS

4.1 Experimental Settings

We use the MovieLens 10M rating data set[3] which is a large-scale movie rating data available for research. In this data, we have around 10 million ratings given by 72,000 users on 10,000 movies. Since this data is big enough, we simply split the data into training and testing set, where the training set is 80% of the whole data. Each user has rated at least 20 movies. We believe these users have rich rating profiles, and black sheep users are not included in this data.

We apply our proposed methodologies on the training set to identify GS users, and examine them by the recommendation performance over the test set. To obtain the prediction errors, we apply UBCF described by Equation 2 as the collaborative filtering recommendation algorithm. In UBCF, we adopt the cosine similarity to measure the user-user similarities, and vary different value of K ($K = 50$ is the besting setting in our experiments) in order to find the best KNN. The recommendation performance is measured by mean absolute error (MAE) which can be depicted by Equation 4.1. R represents the test set, where $|R|$ denotes the total number of ratings in the test set. $R_{a,t}$ is the actual rating given by user a on item t. (a, t) is the <user, item> tuple in the test set. $P_{a,t}$ is the predicted rating by the function in Equation 2. The "abs" function is able to return the absolute value of the prediction error.

$$MAE = \frac{1}{|R|} \sum_{(a,t) \in R} abs(P_{a,t} - R_{a,t}) \qquad (3)$$

4.2 Results and Findings

We follow the four steps in Section 3 to identify the GS users from the training set. As mentioned in the Section 3.2, it is flexible to set different constraints to select good and bad examples. In our experiments, we tried both strict and loose constraints, and we find that we are able to identify more qualified GS users when we use the strict constraints. The strict constraints can be described as follows: we go through the distribution representation matrix, and select the bad examples (i.e., potential GS users) if his or her q1, q2 and mean similarity value is smaller than the first quartile of the q1, q2 and mean distribution of all the users. This group of bad examples is further filtered by the skewness − skewness value smaller than the third quartile of the skewness distribution over all the users will be removed. Finally, we obtain 1,010 bad examples. By applying the loose constraints, we do find more bad examples, but we cannot identify more qualified GS users finally. Therefore, we only present the results based on the strict constraints in the following paragraphs. In terms of the good examples, we select the users whose mean similarity is larger than the third quartile of mean values over all the users. Due to that there are too many

[3]https://grouplens.org/datasets/movielens/10m/

users in the pool, we finally perform a random sampling to use just 20% of these users as the good examples.

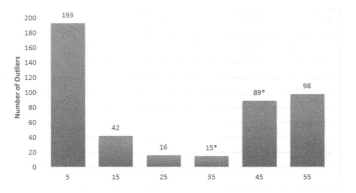

Figure 3: The number of outliers identified by different k values. Note that (*) tells that the two-independent sample statistical test was failed in that setting.

Afterwards, we blend the good and bad examples, and apply the LOF technique to identify the GS users. We tried different values of k and LOF thresholds in our experiments. The number of outliers identified can be shown by Figure 3. For each value of k, we vary the LOF threshold in order to find the largest number of outliers. By using k = 5 and the LOF threshold as 1.34, we are able to identify 193 outliers as the GS users. It is not surprising, since GS users are always a small proportion of the users in the data. In addition, the group of outliers can only be considered as GS users if the MAE of the rating profiles associated with these users is significantly larger than the MAE based on the non-GS users. We use 95% as confidence level, and apply the two-independent sample statistical test to examine whether they meet this requirement. The test failed only when k equals to 35 and 45. As a result, the best setting in our experiment is that k equals 5 and LOF threshold as 1.34, since they help us identify the largest number of qualified GS users.

Table 3: MAE Results

All Users	Good Examples	Bad Examples	Remaining Users	GreySheep Users
0.869	0.868	0.868	0.869	0.908

Table 3 describes the MAE evaluated based on the rating profiles in the test set associated with different groups of the users. The "remaining users" refer to users excluding the identified GS users. There are no statistically differences on MAE values for these user groups if we do not take the group of GS uses into account. In terms of the 193 GS users we find, the MAE value is 0.908. The increase in MAE compared with other group of the users is 4.6%. We further perform a two-independent statistical test on the MAE values by the group of GS users and other group of users, in order to examine whether the result is statistically significant. We use 95% as confidence level, and the statistic test produces p-values smaller than 0.05, which confirms that the MAE by the GS users is

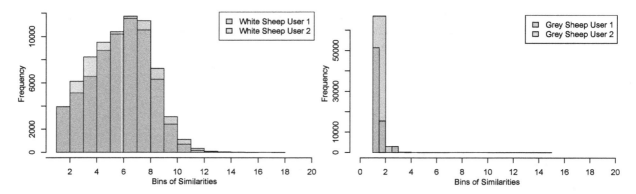

Figure 4: Visualization of the Similarity Distributions

significantly higher. By this way, we confirm the 193 outliers we find can be viewed as GS users.

We look into the characteristics of identified GS and White Sheep users. We select two GS users and two White Sheep users as the representatives, visualize the distribution of user similarities, as shown in Figure 4. The bars in slate blue and coral present the histograms for two users, while the bars in plum capture the overlaps between two histograms. The x-axis is the bins of the similarities, while we put the similarity values (in range [0, 1]) into 20 bins with each bin size as 0.05. The y-axis can tell how many similarity or correlation values that fall in corresponding bins. Note that the distribution based on user similarities for White Sheep users is not the same as the ideal situation described in Figure 1. The reason why is that there are no left-skewed similarity distributions in this data. Most of the user's similarity distributions are shown as normal, slightly right-skewed or heavily right-skewed. From Figure 4, we can clearly observe that most of the correlations between GS users and other users are pretty low, which presents a heavily right-skewed distribution of the similarities. The situation is much better for the White Sheep users, since they usually have highly correlated neighbors. According to the observations at the bins from 15 and 20, we can discover that we have at least 100 high correlations for the White Sheep users, but almost zero for the GS users. This pattern is consistent with the definition of GS and White Sheep users in [10]. According to previous research [6, 10], we need to apply other recommendation algorithms (such as content-based approaches) to reduce the prediction errors for these GS users, where we do not explore further in this paper.

5 CONCLUSIONS

In this paper, we propose a novel approach to identify Grey Sheep users based on the distribution of user similarities or correlations. The proposed approach in this paper is much easier than the previous methods [6, 8, 10] in terms of the complexity. In our future work, we will compare the proposed approach with existing ones to explore whether our approach is significantly better. Furthermore, the same approach can also be used to identify *Grey Sheep items* in addition to the Grey Sheep users.

The problem of Grey Sheep users may not only happen in the traditional recommender systems, but also exist in other types of

the recommender systems. For example, in the context-aware recommender systems [1, 14, 15], the definition of Grey Sheep users could be the users who have unusual tastes in specific contextual situations. The proposed approach in this paper can be easily extended to these special recommender systems, and we may explore it in our future work.

REFERENCES

[1] Gediminas Adomavicius, Bamshad Mobasher, Francesco Ricci, and Alexander Tuzhilin. 2011. Context-Aware Recommender Systems. *AI Magazine* 32, 3 (2011), 67–80.
[2] Markus M Breunig, Hans-Peter Kriegel, Raymond T Ng, and Jörg Sander. 2000. LOF: identifying density-based local outliers. In *ACM sigmod record*, Vol. 29. ACM, 93–104.
[3] Robin Burke. 2002. Hybrid recommender systems: Survey and experiments. *User modeling and user-adapted interaction* 12, 4 (2002), 331–370.
[4] Varun Chandola, Arindam Banerjee, and Vipin Kumar. 2009. Anomaly detection: A survey. *ACM computing surveys (CSUR)* 41, 3 (2009), 15.
[5] Mark Claypool, Anuja Gokhale, Tim Miranda, Pavel Murnikov, Dmitry Netes, and Matthew Sartin. 1999. Combining content-based and collaborative filters in an online newspaper. In *Proceedings of ACM SIGIR workshop on recommender systems*, Vol. 60.
[6] Mustansar Ghazanfar and Adam Prugel-Bennett. 2011. Fulfilling the Needs of Gray-Sheep Users in Recommender Systems, A Clustering Solution. In *Proceedings of the 2011 International Conference on Information Systems and Computational Intelligence*. 18–20.
[7] Mustansar Ali Ghazanfar and Adam Prügel-Bennett. 2014. Leveraging clustering approaches to solve the gray-sheep users problem in recommender systems. *Expert Systems with Applications* 41, 7 (2014), 3261–3275.
[8] Benjamin Gras, Armelle Brun, and Anne Boyer. 2016. Identifying Grey Sheep Users in Collaborative Filtering: a Distribution-Based Technique. In *Proceedings of the 2016 Conference on User Modeling Adaptation and Personalization*. ACM, 17–26.
[9] Victoria Hodge and Jim Austin. 2004. A survey of outlier detection methodologies. *Artificial intelligence review* 22, 2 (2004), 85–126.
[10] John McCrae, Anton Piatek, and Adam Langley. 2004. Collaborative filtering. *http:// www. imperialviolet. org* (2004).
[11] Paul Resnick, Neophytos Iacovou, Mitesh Suchak, Peter Bergstrom, and John Riedl. 1994. GroupLens: an open architecture for collaborative filtering of netnews. In *Proceedings of the 1994 ACM conference on Computer supported cooperative work*. ACM, 175–186.
[12] Manuela Ruiz-Montiel and José Aldana-Montes. 2009. Semantically enhanced recommender systems. In *On the move to meaningful internet systems: OTM 2009 workshops*. Springer, 604–609.
[13] Xiaoyuan Su and Taghi M Khoshgoftaar. 2009. A survey of collaborative filtering techniques. *Advances in artificial intelligence* 2009 (2009), 4.
[14] Y. Zheng, B. Mobasher, and R. Burke. 2014. CSLIM: Contextual SLIM Recommendation Algorithms. In *Proceedings of the 8th ACM Conference on Recommender Systems*. ACM, 301–304.
[15] Yong Zheng, Bamshad Mobasher, and Robin Burke. 2015. Similarity-Based Context-aware Recommendation. In *Proceedings of the 2015 Conference on Web Information Systems Engineering*. Springer Berlin Heidelberg, 431–447.

The Extension and Implementation of the Autonomous Movement Framework

Théo Rivière	Héctor Gutiérrez Ayala	Jeremy Hajek
Graduate Student	Graduate Student	Industry Associate Professor
Illinois Tech	Illinois Tech	Illinois Tech
triviere@hawk.iit.edu	hectorgutierrezayala@gmail.com	hajek@iit.edu

ABSTRACT

The internet changes the way we do business, with companies like Amazon, Uber, and Google reshaping the way commerce is done delivering packages. Companies, such as Nokia, are demonstrating drone fleets being used for public safety over large scale desert areas. Our research asked, could this technology be replicated on a small scale for independent operators to use? The initial goal of this project was to design and develop a framework to control and manage drone fleets for use in search and rescue and disaster relief. We were able to design a platform and framework that integrated common off-the-shelf drones and accessible Windows computers and Android Phones to build and deploy our Autonomous Movement Framework.

Keywords: Autopilot; open-source; Pixhawk; Automation; Rechargeable Batteries Delivery Drone; 3DR Iris; Quadcopter; UAV; Ground Station, Charging Pad; Python; MAVProxy; MAVLink; Mission Planner

1. INTRODUCTION

This paper is an extension of the Autonomous Movement Framework (AMF) research initially presented by Mark Milhouse in 2015[3]. Inspired by the 2012 "Taco Copter hoax [7]," the goal was to create a platform that allowed an autonomously piloted drone to make a delivery using GPS and a mobile phone application.

Though the Taco Copter was an internet hoax, the Autonomous Movement Framework was not. The initial prototype work showed this was feasible with off-the-shelf drones. Mr. Milhouse succeeded in creating the pillars of the framework by having a working application that could allow the drone to drop a package at a required location.

We have seen the Fire Department of New York deploy drones for use in fighting warehouse fires with great success [8]. Our investigations wanted to be able to replicate these abilities through commodity based hardware and software. Since 2015, the AMF project has sought to do just that.

RIIT'17, October 4-7, 2017, Rochester, NY, USA
© 2017 Association for Computing Machinery.
ACM ISBN 978-1-4503-5120-1/17/10...$15.00.
DOI: https://doi.org/10.1145/3125649.3125653

The AMF prototype has been expanded to four units and has built a new field recharging system to allow a quick and autonomous recharging of drone batteries. This paper will focus on the usability of the updated framework and the new charging system.

2. FRAMEWORK
2.1 Hardware components
2.1.1 Drones
For this project, four Unmanned Aerial Vehicles, or UAVs, were used; two 3D Robotics Iris Quadcopters [1] and two DJI F450 Quadcopters [2]. The Iris Quadcopters were chosen for their configurability, their modular build with easily replaceable parts and their durability, despite a limited carrying capacity and travel distance [3].

	3D Robotics Iris Quadcopters	DJI F450 Quadcopter
Battery	5100 mAh 3S 8C lithium polymer battery	5100 mAh 3S 8C lithium polymer battery
Motors	AC 2830, 950 kV	E305 2312E Motor (960kv, CW)
Propellers	IRIS+ Propeller Set (10.5 x 4.7 inches)	9450 Self-tightening Propellers (9.5 x 4.5 inches)
GPS	uBlox GPS with integrated magnetometer	Radiolink SE100 GPS Module for PixHawk
Telemetry	3DR Radio 915mHz	3DR Radio 915mHz

Figure 1: Aircrafts' Specs

2.1.2 Command and control server
Initial work began by augmenting the default software, Mission Planner, used to send our drones flight plans. The goal of this software is to easily perform alterations on the drone's settings and carrying out tests and calibrations. Ubuntu Linux was used on a virtual machine installed on Windows computers to do this. The Linux environment was used because of the compatibility issues that the Mission Planner software had when working on Windows.

However, recent released versions of Mission Planner have considerably diminished the number of compatibility issues and, because of that, the tests can occur on Windows installed computers. This opens our Framework up to be used by the 100s of millions of Windows based computers.

Figure 2: 3D Robotics Iris Quadcopters

Figure 3: DJI F450 Quadcopter with 3D-printed shell

The most recent tests were run on a MSI GS60 6QE running on Windows 10. The server was connected to the drones via a 915 MHz serial radio telemetry transceiver. It was also connected to the internet in order to be able to receive orders from our mobile application. The code and deployment instructions for this software are kept on the project's Github account as we wanted to keep the project always available for access, download, and inspection.

2.1.3 PixHawk

Both types of drones use PixHawk Flight Controller. Pixhawk is an open-hardware project which goal is to provide high-end autopilot hardware [4]. The PixHawk is the core element of this project. The device has a set of inputs and outputs that are connected to the drone flight instruments, allowing to control it and have a feedback of flight data.

2.2 Software Components

2.2.1 PixHawk Firmware

PixHawk Firmware gives the ability to easily modify features of the drone without modifying the source code. Features such as maximum altitude or speed can be altered to adapt the drones to the requirement of the user. This is what allows Mission Planner, for example, to easily interact with the drone. The simplicity of

use of the PixHawk was the main reason the Iris Quadcopter was chosen in the first place, and also the reason why it was used again with the DJI F450 Quadcopter.

2.2.2 MAVProxy and Ground control station

The protocol to communicate between a ground control station and the UAV is what allows many kind of software, such as Mission Planner, to use a common set of functions on different kind of drones. The MAVlink protocol is a common standard of communication written in Python. In order to be able to send flight commands to our drones after sending an order from a phone, MAVproxy had to be modified. The phone app sends the coordinates to the server which then use MAVproxy to send flight data to the PixHawk that controls the drone. In order to simplify the whole process, the server has been designed in Python too. Originally, the server could only handle one drone trip at a time but, after some updates, it is now able to control many UAVs at a time. To do that, the ground station reprograms the single radio's netID to the one corresponding to the desired drone. By this we gain a many to 1 relationship (1 radio to ~500 radios). But in the case of reprogramming netIDs we lose the ability for the drones to use their radio for sending telemetry back to a base station since we are constantly re-programming the based radio's netID, there is nowhere to return and signal too. Solutions for that are being considered today. One would be to have another station on 915 MHz out-of-band, that would collect all broadcasted telemetry for logging purposes and in software we would sort and parse the data.

2.2.3 Mobile Phone Application

The front end of the framework is the phone app. After many iterations and discussion, the application is OpenSource and runs on the Android platform. The app functions in the following way; the client is the mobile phone app, which would be a worker in the field needing a drone to bring equipment to their location. They would launch our app on their phone, upon hitting the "Request Order Now" button, using the Google Maps API, the GPS position of the phone would be sent to the command and control server via the Internet (3G, Wifi, etc.).

Then, as it can be seen in figure 4, a location must be chosen and then, the user must click on "Request order now". A message box will pop up to ask the user to confirm the location. After that, a confirmation message will appear to announce the departure of the drone. The benefit of this method is that the phone's GPS would default to the user's location, but by integrating the Google Maps API, we now give the user the ability to "send" the drone to an area that is a different location, and give the ability for drones to "meet you there." This is a key feature of our Autonomous Movement Fleet.

GPS accuracy varies per device and location, but our target has never been precision accuracy but relative accuracy.

3. THE BATTERY CHARGE

In order to reach the goal of developing an autonomous fleet of drones, many individual aspects of the system have to turn into self-governed features. Along with those aspects, there is the charging process of the quadcopter. This is the most complicated process from an automation standpoint, but the most critical in regard to being able to operate; no battery no flying.

Figure 4: Screenshot of the phone application

3.1 Autonomous charging systems in the market

For solving the non-autonomous charging issue, the first task that has to be done is the research of the current market. Currently, the most common "autonomous charging system" implemented in the market would be the wireless pads for charging mobile devices also known as Qi charging. The charging mechanism is based on inductive charging technology, which allows a pad to charge a compatible phone just by placing it on the charging pad.

The inductive charging system works as follow: the device transfers energy from the charging station to the battery of the phone using electromagnetic induction, which is based in the principle that electricity travelling through a conductor produces a magnetic field around it. This magnetic field can induce current in a wire nearby as long as the wire is inside the range of the field. Besides, the magnetic field is concentrated by coiling the wire, having a more intense field that can easier induce current into the other wire. According to this, in the charging device there would be two wire coils: one for transmitting energy from the pad, and another one to receive the energy at the phone device.

But, apart from the chargers for mobile devices, there are other fields where autonomous charging is used, even if they are not as well-known. For example, Plugless [5] has developed a way of charging electric vehicles wirelessly. This charger adds comfort in the use of electric vehicles; it allows the driver to charge its car by parking on the right spot, where a charging plate is located. No further actions being required.

3.2 Inductive charging vs direct contact

After researching the market products, the following step would be to design the autonomous charger. But, which path would be better to take? The inductive charging or the direct charging? It is true that both of them could work, but there are some advantages and disadvantages related to them that had to be considered:

- Maintenance: with inductive charging, the contact between the parts is reduced. This is an indirect measurement of the wear that the parts would undergo and, thus, the maintenance needed. Furthermore, the inductive charging provides a higher isolation of the components. So, they would be more protected from corrosion or electrical failure and the system would need less maintenance.

- Energy efficiency: the biggest disadvantage related with the inductive charging against the direct contact is that the system is much less efficient than the conventional charger, wasting more energy in the process and needing more time to charge the entire battery.

- Costs: inductive charging tends to be more complex, carrying higher investment costs than the conventional charging system. The energy cost would be higher because of the lower charging efficiency of the inductive technology. However, the costs related to the maintenance, which would be higher for the direct contact, have to be also taken into account.

3.3 The charging mechanism

Both mechanisms have the same main problem: how to place the drone in the exact spot where it is going to be charged? There are basically two ways of placing the quadcopter in the charging spot:

The first option would be to land the UAV directly onto the plug/charging-pad, which, at first glance, is easier in inductive charging than in direct contact. Indeed, the surface covered by the wire coil used for inductive charging is greater than the one covered by a plug used in direct contact. But the commercial GPS margin of error is too large for this operation (4.9 meters) in our framework [9]. If this option is desired to be used, thus, the drone would need to be assisted by some kind of mechanism at the landing time, with the aim of increasing the accuracy of the location of the UAV. One example of assisting the drone would be to add to it a camera and do pattern matching or use computer vision to land or use a physical mechanism in the landing spot that would place the drone in the correct location wherever it lands. At that exact location, even inductive or direct contact could charge the battery.

But, what if it was not necessary to approach the UAV to an exact location, and the drone could land within the GPS margin of error as we have built a modular landing pad that works as a charging pad at a greater size than this margin of error? We would modify the units to contain direct charging plates that could be deployed successfully upon landing and this would be called the Autonomous Charging Framework. Initial provisional patent research is ongoing and is the reason our details here are light.

4 RESULTS

4.1. July 2016 Demo

On July 2016, a demonstration took place at Illinois Institute of Technology to show the proof of concept [6] which was a success. The Iris drones were used for this demo as the DJI F450 were not available during that phase of the project. At this time, it was already possible to fly two different drones on different delivery travels. The demonstration was a success having the AMF manage two independent deliveries. One thing to note, the initial test was done with xBlox GPS receivers, the current research is being undertaken with a newer Radiolink SE100. Consumer GPS has a plus or minus of 5-10 meters. Which the project was willing to trade specific accuracy for usability.

Furthermore, during this demo, two separate antennas were used to control both UAVs. Indeed, it was required to have an antenna for each drone in flight. However, the AMF makes it possible to control several drones with one single reprogrammable antenna.

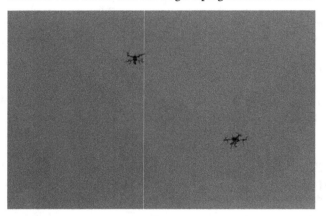

Figure 5: Two drones flying at the same time during July 2016 Demo

4.2. Discussion of test results

4.2.1. Enhancing the framework

Our framework was a success with 2 units showing us that multiple units would be possible. Having multiple autonomous units in the air now brings new challenges.

4.2.2 Air Traffic Control

Theories of management of units in space will need to be developed. While obstacle avoidance and computer vision are suggested starting points, we believe a 3-dimensional pre-programmed grid may be the most efficient way to proceed.
Integration with the FAA when our service is in use would be a critical software piece to provide to them and any local emergency service, via an API.

4.2.3 Transportation

As the number of units increase, the question of how to we box them and ship them? If we have 500 or 5000 or 50000 units? This presents a logistics issue that would need to be further studied. Do we create custom carrying cases? Can we build a custom shipping container? What about an air drop or even a rail-car based way to transport our fleet? These need to be considered and researched.

4.2.4 Manufacturing

Using off-the-shelf drones for the proof of concept has a high cost. Investigation of materials and manufacturing capabilities and economies of scale. Can the drone shells be 3D printed, or stamped aluminum, or another source altogether?

4.2.5 Radio communication security and telemetry collection

A method will need to be devised to be able to collect the telemetry from each drone in the air as it broadcasts and this method will need to be secure to prevent hackers from injecting or broadcasting fake data.

4.2.6. Increasing the automatization

The Autonomous Movement Framework started with the goal to be able to control drone movement. It spawns into fleet management, and now covers fleet control, charging, and deployment. Beyond cheap advertising tricks and delivering pizzas we believe this framework can be used successfully in aiding search and rescue and natural disaster relief but extending human carrying and deployment capabilities.

5 ACKNOWLEDGMENTS

This research would not be possible without the support of Professor Jeremy Hajek, who is the head of the Autonomous Movement Framework project. Along with Jeremy, thanks to the rest of the team for the helping and working along through the different steps of the project, as well as Dr. Krishnamurthy, who has shown interest and has gotten involved in the project.

6 REFERENCES

[1] 3D Robotics https://3dr.com/support/iris/

[2] DJI http://www.dji.com/flame-wheel-arf/feature

[3] Milhouse, M. O. (2015). Framework for Autonomous Delivery Drones. RIIT '15: Proceedings of the 4th Annual ACM Conference on Research in Information Technology, 1-6. [4] PixHawk https://pixhawk.org/

[5] Plugless https://www.pluglesspower.com

[6] Illinois Tech Researchers Demo Drones That Fly Themselves https://www.americaninno.com/chicago/illinois-tech-researchers-demo-drones-that-fly-themselves/

[7] Taco Copter http://tacocopter.com/

[8] FDNY uses drone for first time to help battle a fire http://abcnews.go.com/US/fdny-drone-time-battle-fire/story?id=45971738

[9] http://www.gps.gov/systems/gps/performance/accuracy/

Usability of "Fatchum": A Mobile Application Recipe Recommender System

Zane Myron C. Cruz
College of Computer Studies and
Systems
University of the East
Philippines
zanemyroncruz@gmail.com

Janmel Jerome R. Alpay
College of Computer Studies and
Systems
University of the East
Philippines
janmel.alpay@gmail.com

Joshua Dale D. Depeno
College of Computer Studies and
Systems
University of the East
Philippines
joshuadino@icloud.com

Milaluna Joyce C. Altabirano
College of Computer Studies and
Systems
University of the East
Philippines
joycealtabirano@gmail.com

Rex Bringula
College of Computer Studies and
Systems
University of the East
Philippines
rex_bringula@yahoo.com

ABSTRACT

This study[1] determined the factors that influenced the usability of "Fatchum"—a mobile application Filipino recipe recommender system. Toward this goal, two sets of data were gathered to determine the usability of the mobile app. The first set of data gathered the demographic factors (i.e., age, gender, occupation, level of occupation, and level of knowledge in cooking) and the subjective measures of usability of the app in terms of its design-related factors. The design-related factors were measured in terms of user-interface, navigability, and functionality. It was shown that age, gender, and navigability were significant factors that influenced the usability of the app. The objective measures showed that the app can provide recipe names quickly but fails to share the recipes in a social networking site. Thus, the system is partially successful in meeting its intended purpose. Recommendations for future studies are also offered.

CCS CONCEPTS

• **Human-centered computing→Ubiquitous and mobile computing→Empirical studies in ubiquitous and mobile computing**

KEYWORDS

recipe recommender system; Filipino food; mobile app; usability

RIIT'17, October 4–7, 2017, Rochester, NY, USA
© 2017 Association for Computing Machinery.
ACM ISBN 978-1-4503-5120-1/17/10...$15.00
https://doi.org/10.1145/3125649.3125650

ACM Reference format:

Zane Myron Cruz, Janmel Jerome Alpay, Joshua Dale Depeno, Milaluna Joyce Altabirano, and Rex Bringula. 2017. Usability of "Fatchum": A Mobile Application Recipe Recommender System. In *Proceedings of RIIT, New York, USA, October 2017 (RIIT'17),* 6 pages.
DOI: https://doi.org/10.1145/3125649.3125650

1 INTRODUCTION

People tend to produce food waste [9,22,28] despite global hunger problem [22,31]. Globally, more than 30% of the human food is not consumed [13,14,15] which is more than enough to stop hunger [22]. In the Philippines, it was reported that 15-24.9% of the Filipino population was undernourished [30]. A local study reported that the number of Filipinos who experienced hunger increased from 2.6 million to 3.1 million at the end of December 2016 [26]. Ironically, however, each Filipino wasted 3.29 kg of rice per year [24]. Different studies showed that domestic households are the major contributor of food waste and food losses [2,22].

Household food waste was generated because of behaviors relating to food planning, preparation, storage, and consumption [23]. Households primarily wasted vegetables, cereals, dairy products, and meat [15]. But as Halloran et al. [15] said, improved communications, more efficient food packaging, and better food labels are some of the ways to minimize food waste. Likewise, researchers are offering household techniques to reduce household food waste [7]. For instance, researchers in the field of human-computer interaction are actively addressing the issue of food waste in an attempt that mobile applications can at least change the behavior of people [10,21].

However, there is still an issue in food waste that has not yet been resolved in the current mobile applications. People may have leftover ingredients in preparing their meals. These leftover ingredients may be stored in refrigerators. Smart refrigerators may remind users about what is stored, but people may not know what to do with the ingredients. This study attempted to address tthis gap. Toward this goal, a mobile application named "Fatchum" (which means "by chance" in English) was developed with the goal of recommending Filipino recipes based on all possible combinations of ingredients inputted by the users. Specifically, the study sought to find answers to the following questions: Research Question 1 (RQ1) What are the demographic factors of the participants in terms of age, gender, occupation, and skills in cooking? (RQ2) What are the subjective (i.e., the mobile app-design related factors) and objective measures of usability of the mobile application named "Fatchum"? (RQ3) Do demographic factors and mobile app-design related factors, singly or in combination, influence the usability of "Fatchum"?

2 LITERATURE REVIEW AND HYPOTHESIS

2.1 Food Preparation and Cooking

Aarseth and Olsen [1] investigated the cooking behaviors of 9 Norwegian and 10 Danish couples with full time works. They revealed that three patterns of cooking behaviors emerged from the interviews they conducted with the participants. The first pattern is that food preparation is still the main responsibility of the woman. Couples may both take part in the food preparation but agree that the woman is still in-charge in food preparation. The second pattern is called "man does it his own way." This means that men find easier ways to cook meals whereas women focus more on the quality of the food. Also, the study revealed that men view cooking as a hobby, and not primarily a function of the father. The third pattern is that cooking is joint project of the couples. The couples share common responsibilities of preparing meals for the family or friends.

In a similar study, Szabo [28] pointed out that men and women cook differently. The study consisted of a sample 30 Canadian men who are 26-58 years old, single and married participants, and who cook at home. It was shown that men cook because of practical reasons; they cook when no one is available to cook for them, or when they are more skilled than their partners [4,28]. It was also revealed that men cook because they want to impress women (for single participants), to help their wives (for married participants), and to express love and care for the members of the family. The first finding confirmed the third pattern of cooking described in the study of Aarseth and Olsen [1]. Furthermore, the result of Szabo rejected the popular notion that women cook because they are the ones who take care of the health of the family. The author also found that men cook because they want to contribute to the welfare of the family.

De Backer and Hudders [8] revealed that Belgian women tend to eat more home-cooked meals than men. Conversely, Belgian men have higher tendency to consume ready-to-eat meals than Belgian women. It is also revealed that there are more men than women who eat fast food. In contrast, women are more health-conscious as they eat more fruits and vegetables, and less with salty foods than men. As expected, women cook more often than men. The researchers also found that younger men (below 38 years old) who watch edutainment TV cooking shows were less likely to cook. On the other hand, older men (at least 38 years old) who watch edutainment TV cooking shows were more likely to cook.

2.2 Demographics and Mobile App Usage

The usability of mobile applications can be measured in terms of three factors–its users, the tasks involved in using the application, and the context where the application is utilized [16]. This is called the PACMAD (*People At the Centre of Mobile Application Development*) usability model. According to this model, the physical characteristics and prior experience in using mobile apps should be considered in the development of mobile apps. Mobile devices with limited screen size and input mechanisms may pose challenges to non-experts and people with physical challenges (e.g., unclear eye vision).

The PACMAD model advocates that the mobile app is usable if the mobile app could meet the desired goals of the users within the context of use. Context of use refers to "the environment in which the user will use the application" (p. 3). The environment may refer to the physical location where the mobile application is utilized or to "other features such as the user's interaction with other people or objects and other tasks the user may be trying to accomplish" (p. 4). For example, if a mobile app is intended to motivate its users to have a light walk (e.g., PokemonGo), then the context of use involves the physical environment and the features of the app.

The factors proposed by the Harrison et al. [16] are suitable to this study. Cooking, as previously shown by different studies [1,8,28], might be influenced by age, gender, occupation, and cooking skills. Similarly, the use of a mobile cooking application like "Fatchum" might also be influenced by the demographic factors, tasks to be carried out, and context of use. Thus, it is hypothesized that (H1) *demographic factors of the participants in terms of age, gender, occupation, and skills in cooking influence the usability of "Fatchum".*

2.3 Subjective Measures of Usability

Usability is defined as the "extent to which a product can be used by specified users to achieve specified goals with effectiveness, efficiency and satisfaction in a specified context of use" [19]. Efficiency refers to the resources spent in performing tasks while effectiveness refers to the ability of users to complete tasks using a technology with the assurance that the output of that task has quality. Satisfaction, on the other hand, is the subjective evaluation of users based on content in using the technology.

Subjective and objective measures are two general ways to measure usability [5,11,17]. The subjective measures involve asking or requesting the participants to rate the dimensions of usability of a system using a survey form [5,17]. The dimensions of usability may vary from one study to another [5] since usability has no universal definition [25]. Furthermore, the type of device may influence the usability of the software [3]. For example, Kortum and Sorber [20] investigated whether system usability scale (SUS) scores varied across platforms (android phones, android tablets, and iPads). They showed that there is a significant relationship between length of prior user experience of top 10 apps and SUS scores for tablet users [20].

Recently, there were studies that investigated the usability of mobile applications [3,17]. Billi et al. [3, p. 339] pointed out that accessibility and usability studies regarding mobile applications are necessary because the platform (e.g., mobile phones) of this software provide "ubiquitous access, portability, more personal than personal computer, democratization of information access, opportunistic interaction, and reduced complexity". The authors proposed that mobile applications should have mechanisms where users can find the content of the app, make the users familiar with it, and navigate through it. Similarly, the study of Hoehle and Venkatesh [17] proposed six dimensions of usability of mobile apps. These dimensions are application design, application utility, user interface graphics, user interface input, user interface output, and user interface structure. Based on these studies, it is hypothesized that (H2) *the perceived mobile app design-related factors in terms of user-interface, navigability, and functionality influence the usability of "Fatchum".*

2.4 Objective Measures of Usability

Objective measures of usability are conducted to augment the subjective measures of usability. According to Hornbaek [18], and Brooks and Hestness [6], objective measures are independent from the perceptions of the users because the actual outcomes are measured. Filippi and Barattin [11] included task duration, task accuracy, completeness, effectiveness, efficiency, dead time, productiveness, error rate, number of errors, recovery time, help system usage, expert help, used commands/features, unused comments/features, critical statements ratio, sidetracking, training time, learning rate, and cognitive workload. Bringula [5] utilized time to complete the tasks and the success rate in assessing the web portal usability.

In the current study, searching for the name of recipes, searching for ingredients, and sharing the recipe in *Facebook* are the indicators of objective measures. Based on the above studies, the study adopted the objective measures of usability in terms of time spent in completing the tasks and the success rate of completing the tasks.

3 RESEARCH FRAMEWORK

Figure 1 shows the research framework of the study. The independent variables include the demographic factors of the participants and their perceptions on the mobile app design-related factors of the mobile application. The demographic factors of the participants include age, gender, occupation, and level of knowledge in cooking. Occupation indicates whether the participants of the study are employed or not. The level of knowledge in cooking intends to assess the participants' experience in cooking.

The mobile app design-related factors are measured in terms of user-interface, navigability, and functionality. User-interface measures the overall design of the mobile app. Navigation is about ease of moving from one interface to another one. Functionality measures the ability of the mobile app to meet the objectives of the participants. Lastly, the usability of the mobile app is measured in terms of satisfaction of use.

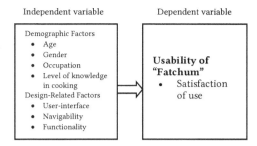

Figure 1: Research Framework of the Study

4 METHODOLOGY

4.1 Description of the Software Utilized

"Fatchum" is an android-based mobile application recipe recommender system (Figure 2-a). It includes usual searching of recipe by its name (Search by Recipe Name). The application also accepts ingredients from the users and finds all possible recipes that match the ingredients (Search by Ingredients; see Figure 2-b). For example, if the user inputs pork, soy sauce, and vinegar (Figure 2-b), these three ingredients can be found in the pork *adobo*, and in pork and *kangkong guisado* (stewed river spinach); two ingredients in *binagoongang baboy* (pork with fermented krill), etc. (Figure 2-c). The user can tap the recipe for more information. The internal database of the app contains 500 Filipino recipes. Users may also input the recipe they invented in the app and may share it in a social networking site (SNS). This task is called Share Recipe.

Figure 2. (a) Home Screen of "Fatchum", (b) Search Recipe by Ingredients, (c) Search Results (*images of recipes not included*)

4.2 Research Locale, Sample Size, and Sampling Design

The study was conducted in three local communities in Metro Manila where the researchers reside. According to informal interviews with the local officials, there are 300 households in the first community, 500 in the second community and 250 in the third community. They purposively selected because it was perceived that their own local communities must be the first to benefit from the mobile application. The local communities belong to a first-class urban area and to a middle-income class sector [29].

A sample size of 91 participants was computed with the following parameters: anticipated effect size = 0.35, power level = 0.95, number of predictors = 7 and probability level = 0.01)

[27]. Participants were selected by choosing every three house starting from the community hall. It was decided to select 120 participants (40 participants on each local community) to increase the chance of achieving the desired sample size. One hundred participants agreed to participate in the experiment.

4.3 Research Design, Data Gathering Procedure, and Statistical Treatment of Data

This correlational research determined whether the demographic factors of the participants and subjective measures of mobile app design-related factors could influence usability of the mobile app "Fatchum". The study involved two phases. The first phase involved the administration of the survey instrument. Subjective measures of usability and the demographic factors of the participants were the first set of data gathered. After the three-day intervention period (i.e., the use of the mobile application), participants were asked to rate the mobile app design-related factors in terms of user interface, navigability, and functionality. The second phase commenced after all survey forms were retrieved.

In the second phase, objective measures were collected through experimental methods. Thirty participants were selected from the 100 participants. One of the three local communities was randomly selected. Participants were given five tasks to complete wherein they have to locate two recipes by its names, locate one recipe with two ingredients, and post one recipe they have made in *Facebook*. The time spent doing these activities were collected. The task-provider gave the participants the task to be completed. Meanwhile, an observer recorded the length of time the participants spent in doing the tasks. The participants would inform the observer that they already completed the task. Participants were informed that they may not complete the tasks and may leave the experiment anytime they want to. Interviews were conducted to determine their experiences in using the application. The two phases of data gathering lasted for two months. Informal interviews were conducted to further explain the results of the study.

The focus of the present study was on the satisfaction of use of the mobile app. The study did not investigate whether the mobile app was successful in reducing household waste. Furthermore, it did not determine whether the participants of the study followed the recipes that the system recommended.

A survey form was utilized as the research instrument of the study. Two researchers in usability studies and one Information Technology industry practitioner validated the content of the questionnaire in terms of appropriateness of the factors and clarity of the items. After two rounds of revisions, the final survey form was achieved. Afterwards, the survey form was pilot-tested to 40 participants of one community who were excluded in the study. The first part of the questionnaire asked the participants about their age, gender, occupation, and level of knowledge in cooking (1 – Not skilled to 5 – Highly skilled). The Likert scale, mean range, and verbal interpretation are shown in Table 1.

The second part was about the assessment of the participants on the design-related factors of the mobile app in terms of user-interface, navigability, and functionality. Participants can answer the items using the scale of 1 (strongly disagree) to 5 (strongly agree).

Table 1. Scale, Mean Range, and Verbal Interpretation

Scale	Mean Range	Verbal Interpretation
1	1.00 – 1.50	Strongly disagree / Highly unskilled /Very unsatisfied
2	1.51– 2.50	Disagree / Unskilled / Unsatisfied
3	2.51– 3.50	Somewhat (agree / skilled / satisfied)
4	3.51– 4.50	Agree / Skilled / Satisfied
5	4.51– 5.00	Strongly agree/Highly skilled/Highly Satisfied

The study used descriptive statistics such as mean, frequency, and percentage. Multiple regression analysis at 5% level of probability and 95% reliability was employed to determine which of the demographic and the design-related factors influence the usability of the mobile app.

5 RESULTS

RQ1: Demographics of Participants, and RQ2: Subjective and Objective Measures of Usability

The participants of the study are relatively young (M = 32.3 years old). Almost a quarter of the participants of the study are female (f = 73, 73%). Majority of the participants are working (f = 58, 58%). It can also be noted that most of the female participants are housewives (f = 40, 40%). Participants rated their knowledge in cooking as "moderately skilled" (M = 3.21).

Participants agreed that "Fatchum" had a good interface design (M = 3.85). They also agreed that the application is easy to navigate (M = 3.98). Of the three design-related factors, functionality (M = 4.13) got the highest mean rating. This indicates that the app received favorable ratings in terms of subjective measures (overall M = 3.97). However, participants are only somewhat satisfied (M = 3.25) with the app.

Sharing recipe is the most difficult task to accomplish (M = 225.80 sec). None of the 30 participants were able to share their recipes in *Facebook*. This can be attributed to the slow Internet connection in the area. This is a national problem since the Philippines has the slowest Internet connection in Asia [12]. Nonetheless, the participants were able to locate recipes by names (M = 17.3 sec; 100% completion rate) or by ingredients (M = 79.6 sec; 100% completion rate). This is because locating recipes is internally stored in the database of the mobile phone and this task does not require Internet connection. Searching for the name of recipes was the quickest task completed. Three participants recommended that the database of the app be improved by including other recipes of other nationalities.

RQ 3: Influence of Demographic Factors and Mobile App-Design Related Factors on Usability of "Fatchum"

Table 2 shows the regression of demographic factors and mobile app design-related factors on satisfaction of use of "Fatchum". It shows that age, gender, and navigability are the factors that influence usability of "Fatchum". Navigability is the strongest predictor of usability of "Fatchum" while Gender has a negative impact on the usability of the app. The three variables were able to explain 94% of the variability of the usability of the app. The regression results are unlikely to have arisen from sampling error ($F(3,97)$ = 527.98, $p < 0.05$).

Table 2. Regression of Demographic Factors and Mobile App Design-Related Factors on Satisfaction of Use of "Fatchum"

Variables	Beta	Sig.
Age	0.35	0.001
Gender	-0.07	0.016
Occupation	-0.02	0.543
Knowledge on Cooking	-0.07	0.511
Functionality	0.21	0.366
User Interface	0.29	0.125
Navigability	0.66	0.000

Adj. R^2 = 0.941
$F(3,97)$ = 527.98
Sig. = 0.000

6 DISCUSSION

This study determined the factors that influence the usability of a mobile cooking application named "Fatchum". The participants of the study are relatively young and are on the early stage of building a family. Most of the participants of the study are female and are housewives. The findings indicate that women are the ones preparing the food for the family. This is consistent with the study of Aarseth and Olsen [1] which maintained the women are primarily in charge in cooking. Nonetheless, there are 27 male participants that said that they also cook. Informal interviews revealed that men perceived that cooking is a shared responsibility in the household. This is consistent with the studies of Aarseth and Olsen [1], and Szabo [28]. Participants perceived that they were only moderately skilled in cooking. This can be attributed to the fact that they have just started building their own families and that they are still learning to cook on their own.

Participants agreed that "Fatchum" has a good user interface design. This is because the design of the app is straightforward. With only few taps (2-3 taps), users can already find the name of the recipe and the recipe ingredients. It is also easy to transfer from one screen to another screen. It is worth noting that the app received highest rating in terms of functionality. This finding suggests that the app is able to respond to the queries of the users. It can also accurately match the inputted ingredients with the possible recipes that require such ingredients. Thus, the app received favorable ratings from the participants.

It is easier to search a recipe through its name than to search a recipe by ingredients. This can be attributed to the fact that users executing the first task already know the name of the recipe to cook, but not necessarily know how to prepare it. In other words, they already know the name of the recipe to search for. On the other hand, searching recipes through the possible combinations of all ingredients will take time. The app can provide all possible recipes that use the ingredients that the user supplied. When the results of the query are presented, users still need to tap each recipe and decide which one to prepare. This explains the disparity in the time spent between the two tasks.

However, despite of its good user-interface design, easy navigation, and acceptable functionalities, users are not fully satisfied with the app. The last task carried out by the participants may explain this inconsistency. The last objective measure is to determine the time spent sharing the recipe in a SNS. It took the participants almost 4 minutes to do the task and none of them were successful in completing the task. As a result, participants are not fully satisfied with the app.

The implications of the results are twofold. First, subjective measures may not fully explain the usability of a system. In the case of this study, despite having good survey evaluation results in terms of design factors of the mobile app, the satisfaction of use is only marginal. The items of the questionnaire may not capture the whole picture of the usability of the app. Thus, the second implication is that objective measures are necessary to further explain the results of subjective measures. Hence, it is recommended that both subjective and objectives measures be incorporated in future usability studies.

The results of the regression analysis show that two demographic factors and one of mobile app design-related factor influenced the satisfaction of use of "Fatchum". These factors are able to explain 94% in the variability of satisfaction of use of "Fatchum". Therefore, age, gender, and navigability are good predictors of satisfaction of use of mobile cooking app. It is also concluded that the data of the study partially supported the first and second hypotheses.

Navigability is the strongest predictor of satisfaction of use. This supports the study of Billi et al. [3]. The result suggests that mobile apps should present the outputs of user queries in just few taps (2-3 taps). It also implies that mobile apps should be designed in such a way that users will not get lost while using the apps. These design considerations challenge mobile app designers due to limited physical capacity of mobile devices. In order to meet the challenges, user's tasks must be accomplished in just few steps.

Informal interviews with one female and male participants were conducted to explain why gender has negative impact on the usability of the mobile app. The female participant said that this could be explained by the reason that males as cooks are not meticulous about the way they prepare their food. Men prepare the family meal as long as the ingredients are safe and readily available. The male participant corroborated this statement. According to the male participant, the app provides the complete listing of ingredients based on the search query. However, he may not follow the ingredients and the preparation of the recommended meal because of time constraints. Instead, male cooks tend to draw their knowledge in cooking from personal experience and cook whatever ingredients are available.

The interview results are in agreement with the result of the study of Aarseth and Olsen [1] that men have their "own way of cooking" food. This finding suggests that food preparation or cooking behaviors of men and women may influence the use of the mobile cooking app. This study revealed that cooking behavior may influence the usability of the app. However, this study did not quantify the strength of this behavior. Future studies may shed light on this research gap.

7   Conclusions, Limitations, and Recommendations

This study determined if the demographic factors of the participants and the subjective measure of mobile app-design related factors influence the usability of the mobile app named "Fatchum". On the basis of the findings presented in the earlier section, the first and second hypotheses are both partially rejected. Age, gender, and ease of navigation (i.e., navigability) were found significant predictors of usability of the mobile app. Navigability had the strongest influence on the satisfaction of use of the mobile cooking app.

Gender had negative influence on the satisfaction of use of the mobile cooking app. While this study revealed that gender had an impact on the usability of the mobile cooking app, the quantitative impact of the cooking behaviors of men and women it is still unclear. Thus, it is recommended that cooking behaviors be incorporated in future studies. This variable may explain the remaining variability not captured in the present study.

The study only considered couples who were relatively young. Hence, the findings may be different from a different age group or marital status. For example, single men or women might prefer to eat fast food or may prepare ready-to-eat meals than to prepare food. In turn, this might influence the use of the mobile app. Other demographic variables such as number of children and household income may also contribute to explaining the usability of the mobile app. It is also recommended that other recipes be incorporated in the mobile app.

The study did not investigate the impact of mobile application on reducing food waste. This will be based on whether the participants of the study followed the recipe recommended by the mobile app and the actual ingredients used as recommended by the mobile app. Thus a follow-up study is recommended. Lastly, the setting of the study may also be considered. It is recommended that future studies may choose a location where the Internet connection is relatively fast.

ACKNOWLEDGMENTS

The authors are indebted to Dr. Mila Arias, to the participants of the study, and to the local community officials. This study is funded by the University of the East.

REFERENCES

[1]   Aarseth, H., and Olsen, B. M. 2008. Food and masculinity in dual-career couples. *Journal of Gender Studies*, 17, 4, 277-287.

[2]   Ambler-Edwards, S., Bailey, K., Kiff, A., Lang, T., Lee, R., Marsden, T., Simons, D., and Tibbs, H. 2014. *Food futures:Rethinking UK Strategy*. Available at http://www.futurelens.com/wp-content/uploads/2014/04/Food-Futures-Rethinking-UK-Strategy.pdf

[3]   Billi, M., Burzagli, L., Catarci, T., Santucci, G., Bertini, E., Gabbanini, F., and Palchetti, E. 2010. A unified methodology for the evaluation of accessibility and usability of mobile applications. *Universal Access in the Information Society*, 9, 4, 337-356.

[4]   Bove, C. and Sobal, J., 2006. Foodwork in newly married couples: making family meals. *Food, Culture & Society*, 9, 1, 70–89.

[5]   Bringula, R. P. 2016. Factors affecting web portal information services usability: A canonical correlation analysis. *International Journal of Human–Computer Interaction*, 32, 10, 814-826.

[6]   Brooks, P., & Hestness, B. (2010). User measures of quality of experience: Why being objective and quantitative is important. *IEEE Network*, 24, 2,8–13.

[7]   Brown, T., Hipps, N. A., Easteal, S., Parry, A., and Evans, J. A. 2014. Reducing domestic food waste by freezing at home. *International Journal of Refrigeration*, 40, 362-369.

[8]   De Backer, C. J., and Hudders, L. 2016. Look who's cooking: Investigating the relationship between watching educational and edutainment TV cooking shows, eating habits and everyday cooking practices among men and women in Belgium. *Appetite*, 96, 494-501.

[9]   EU Fusions. 2016. *Food losses and food waste*. Available at http://data.consilium.europa.eu/doc/document/ST-10730-2016-INIT/en/pdf

[10] Farr-Wharton, G., Choi, J. H. J., and Foth, M. 2014. Food talks back: exploring the role of mobile applications in reducing domestic food wastage. In *Proceedings of the 26th Australian Computer-Human Interaction Conference on Designing Futures: the Future of Design* (Sydney, New South Wales, Australia, December 02-05, 2014). OzCHI '14. ACM, New York, NY, 352-361.

[11] Filippi, S. and Barattin, D. 2012. Generation, adoption, and tuning of usability evaluation Multimethods.*International Journal of Human-Computer Interaction*,28, 6,406-422,

[12] Flores, H. 2017. *At 4.5mpbs, Philippines internet Asia-Pacific slowest*. Available at http://www.philstar.com/headlines/2017/05/23/1702633/4.5-mbps-philippines-internet-asia-pacifics-slowest

[13] Garcia-Garcia, G., Woolley, E., Rahimifard, S., Colwill, J., White, R., and Needham, L. 2016. A methodology for sustainable management of food waste. *Waste and Biomass Valorization*, 1-19.

[14] Griffin, M., Sobal, J., and Lyson, T. A. 2009. An analysis of a community food waste stream. *Agriculture and Human Values*, 26, 1-2, 67-81.

[15] Halloran, A., Clement, J., Kornum, N., Bucatariu, C., and Magid, J. 2014. Addressing food waste reduction in Denmark. *Food Policy*, 49, 294-301.

[16] Harrison, R., Flood, D., and Duce, D. 2013. Usability of mobile applications: literature review and rationale for a new usability model. *Journal of Interaction Science*, 1, 1, 1-16.

[17] Hoehle, H., and Venkatesh, V. 2015. Mobile Application Usability: Conceptualization and Instrument Development. *MIS Quarterly*, 39, 2, 435-472.

[18] Hornbaek, K. (2006). Current practice in measuring usability: Challenges to usability studies and research. *International Journal of Human–Computer Studies*, 64, 79–102.

[19] International Standard Organization (ISO). 1997. ISO 9241-11: Ergonomic requirements for office work with Visual Display Terminals (VDTs): Guidance on usability specification and measures (Part 11). Available at http://www.iso.org/iso/catalogue_detail.htm?csnumber=16883

[20] Kortum, P., and Sorber, M. 2015. Measuring the usability of mobile applications for phones and tablets. *International Journal of Human-Computer Interaction*, 31, 8, 518-529.

[21] Lim, V., Funk, M., Marcenaro, L., Regazzoni, C., and Rauterberg, M. 2017. Designing for action:An evaluation of Social Recipes in reducing food waste. *International Journal of Human-Computer Studies*, 100, 18-32.

[22] Melikoglu, M., Lin, C. S. K., and Webb, C. 2013. Analysing global food waste problem: pinpointing the facts and estimating the energy content. *Central European Journal of Engineering*, 3, 2, 157-164.

[23] Quested, T. E., Parry, A. D., Easteal, S., Swannell, R., 2011. Food and drink waste from households in the UK. *Nutrition Bulletin*, 36, 460–467.

[24] Senate of the Philippines. 2016. *An act providing for a system of redistributing and recycling food waste to promote food security*. Available at https://www.senate.gov.ph/lisdata/2455321128!.pdf

[25] Sindhuja, P. N., and Dastidar, S. G. 2009. Impact of the factors influencing website usability on user satisfaction. *The IUP Journal of Management Research*, 8, 12, 54–66.

[26] Social Weather Stations. 2016. *Second quarter 2016 Social Weather Survey: hunger is 15.2% of families; moderate hunger 13.2%, severe hunger 2.0%*. Available at https://www.sws.org.ph/swsmain/artcldisppage

[27] Soper, D. 2017. *A-priori sample size calculator for multiple regression*. Available at http://www.danielsoper.com/statcalc/calculator.aspx?id=1

[28] Szabo, M. 2014. Men nurturing through food: Challenging gender dichotomies around domestic cooking. *Journal of Gender Studies*, 23,1,18-31.

[29] Wikipedia.org. 2017. Rodriquez, Rizal. Retrieved from https://en.wikipedia.org/wiki/Rodriguez,_Rizal

[30] World Food Programme. 2015. *Hunger map 2015*. Available at http://documents.wfp.org/stellent/groups/public/documents/communications/wfp275057.pdf?_ga=1.248681479.1057544155.1491722844

[31] World Food Programme. 2017. *Zero hunger*. Available at http://www1.wfp.org/zero-hunger

Indexing Architecture for File Extraction from Network Traffic

Pei-Ting Lee
Purdue University
Computer and Information Technology
USA
lee2521@purdue.edu

Baijian Yang
Purdue University
Computer and Information Technology
USA
byang@purdue.edu

ABSTRACT

As crimes, along with nearly every aspect of life, continue to transit into cyberspace, network traffic becomes an increasingly important source of evidence for forensic investigators. Network forensics is most commonly used in analyzing network traffic, identifying suspicious patterns and tracing the source of attack. This paper takes a different approach and views network traffic not as a means to an end, but the source from which evidence can be extracted. When criminals take extra measures to wipe evidence from all physical servers and disks, carving the files from network traffic may become critical to investigations. However, with limitations in current computing power, analyzing each packet for extractable evidence is impractical. This study proposes an architecture for file extraction that incorporates network flow aggregation and indexing for faster, more efficient packet and file extraction.

KEYWORDS

Network traffic, file extraction, flow aggregation, indexing

1 INTRODUCTION

Ever since the Internet's introduction to the general public, it has been gaining users and integrating into everyday lives in a way few other inventions have ever accomplished before. Nowadays, it is hard to find someone who doesn't use the Internet. Criminals are no exceptions. Computers and the Internet are becoming both targets and tools for criminals. Previously inaccessible materials, such as child pornography, could be found relatively easily using the Internet. Hacking into other systems and stealing privileged information has also been made easier and less risky. Meeting like-minded individuals and learning from each other can lead to catastrophic consequences in the cases of people with ill intentions [1]. Because of this,

RIIT'17, October 4-7, 2017, Rochester, NY, USA
© 2017 Association for Computing Machinery.
ACM ISBN 978-1-4503-5120-1/17/10...$15.00.
DOI: http://dx.doi.org/10.1145/3125649.3125655

criminal investigations are increasingly moving into the realm of cyberspace, and among this is the investigation of network traffic.

Network forensics is the field under digital forensics that deals with analyzing network traffic. It involves capturing, recording, and analyzing network traffic in order to reconstruct network activities and discover the identity of the attacker [2]. Other than providing important clues that help investigators trace the attack, network traffic, especially the packets themselves, can also be another source of evidence. For example, if a person obtained a file with critical information from an online source, but no evidence of that file was found on any servers or disks related to the suspect and the source, forensic investigators could reconstruct the file from network packets captured. This usually involves two steps, identifying the target packets and carving the file from the packet payloads.

To fully utilize the network as a source of evidence collection, law enforcement can capture network traffic at strategic locations and extract all files transferred, providing a backup of evidence independent of remote servers and personal storage devices. This sounds enticing to investigators. However, even assuming no encryption on the network traffic, extracting files from network packets faces other difficulties. With the amount of network traffic through critical interfaces, it is extremely difficult to process and analyze all the packets, not to mention carve the files from them as they go through. Faced with this challenge, this study proposes a new architecture that makes packet analysis and file extraction more efficient by utilizing an indexing system with properties from the network traffic.

2 PREVIOUS WORK

2.1 Network Packet Analysis

Network forensics consists of capturing, recording, and analyzing network traffic. Logs and data are collected and analyzed for characteristics, the results of which can be used to trace back to perpetrators. Network packets play an important role in network forensics, serving as the most important, or only, source of evidence.

Network packet analysis can be divided into four types, protocol, packet, flow, and high level traffic analysis [3]. Protocol analysis consists of identifying the protocol and interpreting the communications structures. It mainly uses port numbers, and identifying the function of the source or destination servers to deduce the type of protocol used. Identifying the type of protocol is useful because different protocols can often be used to infer the nature and purpose of the packets.

Packet analysis looks at the individual packets themselves. This includes the actual payload and all the information in single packets. Pattern matching and finding signatures are the most common aspects to packet analysis, and is often used by investigators and researchers in identifying suspicious traffic. Analyzing packet payload and matching signatures are frequently used in finding malware or special types of traffic such as peer-to-peer packets. For example, malware can be classified based on printable strings contained in them [4]. Working with unpacked malware, the researchers' classification technique used string information as a feature vector. Printable strings were extracted from the executable, and a subset of them were selected as features. These features were then used in five different classification algorithms and the results developed into a 5-fold cross-validation test. Their results showed strings from library code, rather than the malware itself, can be used to classify malware into different families.

Another example is Sen, Spatscheck, and Wang's proposed method in [4] that identifies P2P traffic based on the application signatures found in the payload of data packets. Potential signatures of P2P applications were developed by available information from documentations as well as information obtained from analyzing packet-level traces. For example, the BitTorrent protocol starts with a handshake between two peers, followed by a never-ending stream of length-prefixed messages. The authors found that there is a common header in the header of BitTorrent handshake messages. The first byte in the TCP payload is a fixed character with value "19", it is then followed by a 19-byte string, the value of which is "BitTorrent protocol."

Identifying the nature of the packet would then allow investigators to know whether there are files or data that can be extracted from those packets. For example, since P2P systems are used largely for file sharing, identifying P2P packets would allow investigators to collect them and reconstruct the files being transferred. However, even though packet analysis using pattern matching give low false positive results, looking and analyzing each packet requires a lot of resource and computing power, is a burden to network equipment, and takes a long time [6].

Another method frequently utilized to look for malicious traffic is flow analysis. This includes the information obtained by the header, such as source and destination IP and ports. Unlike packet analysis, which looks at individual packets, flow analysis examines related groups of packets. A single communication between server and clients usually consists of many packets, as requests and data are broken down to send over the network. To understand the full conversation between a server and client, it is necessary to look at the whole flow. Flow analysis identifies patterns in packets that show them to be from the same flow and extracts them. With packets grouped according to their flows, data extraction and reconstruction would be possible [3].

Because of the integral role flows play in understanding network traffic, it is often used in identifying different kinds of traffic.

An example of using flow analysis to differentiate peer-to-peer traffic is shown in [7]. The authors classify traffic by only observing host behavior at transport layer. In this study, only the IP address and ports in the transport layer are collected. The port numbers are treated as indexes without any application related information, they are simply used to count the number of distinct ports used by hosts. The behavior of hosts is classified at three levels: social, functional, and application. After parsing the flows, the number of hosts each host interacts with, as well as the number of distinct IP addresses and port numbers used are counted. Using these information, the authors were able to classify the flows according to host behavior.

Flow analysis provides some advantages over packet analysis. The information required for flow analysis is faster and easier to collect, and takes less time and space to store. However, the results are less reliable since it's less transparent than scrutinizing the contents of each packet.

Lastly, high level traffic analysis is looking at traffic from a higher level, for example, identifying HTTP, SMTP traffic, and knowing what kinds of data and protocols they use. Knowing the type of data typically transferred by different kinds of traffic allows investigators to filter packets from which files or other information may be extracted.

2.2 Network Investigation Models

The versatile nature of network traffic makes it hard to define a standard procedure when it comes to investigating networks. There have been numerous proposals of different investigation models that can be applied to network forensics. After reviewing many previously proposed network forensics process models, a generic process model including nine steps can be defined [2]. The nine stages are preparation, detection, incident response, collection, preservation, examination, analysis, investigation, and presentation. In the examination phase, network traces collected from strategically deployed sensors are integrated and fused to form one large data set where analysis can be performed. Moreover, the data is cleaned for redundant information and overlapping time zones. The analysis phase searches, classifies, and correlates indicators to find and match attack patterns. The attack patterns are then put together, reconstructed, and replayed to understand the attacker's intention and how the attack was conducted. The source of attack is then traced during the investigation stage [2].

Most network forensics models and procedures are static and analyses pre-collected data. Gathering and saving evidence in real-time dynamically allows for more efficient evidence collection, especially while the attack is still happening [8]. In the model proposed in [8], a Forensic Server, Detector-Agent, Forensics-Agent, and Response-Agent were deployed. The Detector-Agent analyses real-time network data for signs of intrusion. If found, it notifies the Forensics-Agent, who then collects the digital evidence, creates a digital signature and sends it to the Forensic Server which analyzes the attack pattern. This method gathers attack evidence and response as soon as an intrusion occurs.

In [9], the authors described a system which balanced disk-bandwidth, CPU capacity, and data-reduction that can simultaneously monitor multiple protocols. Because of the redundancy in network data, this system filters packets at the network interface, only capturing significant information and discards all else to lessen the load on the monitors' CPU. The filtered packets were sent to different modules based on their protocol, and protocol-features are extracted in real-time from the reassembled flows, and saved to log buffer. This architecture of a network monitor is efficient in identifying the properties and network activities in real-time, but by only collecting information and discarding for example, data of a retrieved object, it would not be able to support file carving from the packet payload later.

3 ARCHITECTURE

3.1 Motivation

Most studies focus on identifying suspicious data or activity from the network. Although this is an important feature in file extraction from network traffic, as identifying the type of packet is essential to knowing whether there is data to be extracted, it is not the main purpose of this study. In this study, network traffic is viewed as the target to which evidence files can be obtained, not simply the means to which some other source can be traced. Previous studies, whether they use packet or flow analysis, look for signatures that indicate suspicious or malicious traffic. The packets of interest of this study do not necessarily fall under those categories. A simple document with a name written in it may not alert any network intrusion protocols, or any systems looking for suspicious traffic, but it just might be critical to criminal investigations.

For this reason, this study proposes an architecture for file extraction from network traffic alone. Typically, file extraction from network traffic would require a few necessary steps. First, the network packets have to be captured. Then, the packets are organized into flows, and finally, the files are carved from these flows [3]. During the packet capture step, packet analysis, as previously mentioned, would have to be used to determine the contents of the packet—whether or not it is transferring a file that can be extracted. This would require real-time packet analysis which as previously stated, consumes significant amounts of resources and time. This would be impractical to implement in real-world scenarios with large amounts of network traffic every second. Because of this, in the architecture proposed, an extra real-time aggregation and extraction step is added to bypass packet analysis at the time of capture, while at the same time collect enough information to increase the efficiency in packet analysis and file carving later.

3.2 Design

This architecture aims to combine the speed of flow analysis with the accuracy of deep packet analysis, and is shown in Fig. 1.

It mainly consists of six stages: *a)* Collect network traffic, *b)* Dump all collected packets to a database for future file carving and, *c)* Aggregate and extract flow information, *d)* Index flow information obtained, *e)* Use index to obtain necessary packets from the database, and finally, *f)* Reconstruct files from packet payload.

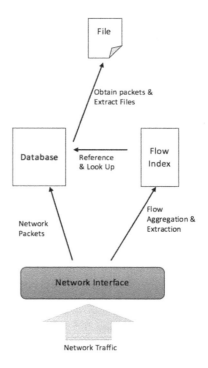

Figure 1: Proposed architecture for efficient file extraction from network traffic. Packets captured at the network interface are stored straight to the database while also saving the aggregated flow properties to the index database.

First of all, devices are placed at strategic locations to capture all network traffic. As the packets are collected at the network interface, they are saved straight into a database, no packet analysis is being conducted at the interface. Instead, network flow information is collected at the network interface. Collecting and processing network flow information requires considerably less resources and time than deep packet analysis, as the information needed are mostly obtainable from the header. Flows are aggregated and saved in a buffer at the network interface in real-time. As soon as each flow comes to an end, the overall properties of that flow are extracted and written to a separate database. This second database is used as the flow index. Properties written to the flow index include source and destination IP address, source and destination port numbers, duration of the whole flow, total number of packets in the flow, total number of bytes transferred, start and end time of the flow, and any file names that appeared in each flow.

In other words, the flow index database stores all metadata of each flow that passes through the network interface, obtained by flow aggregation done at the interface. Taking computing power into consideration, the computing at the network interface is kept to a minimum, only involving flow aggregation and extraction of the key elements of their properties. The flow index is then used as a look up table to acquire the corresponding packets from the database. Once the packets are obtained, files can be carved out and reconstructed from the payload.

The information from each flow used to construct the flow index are all indicators to the nature and contents of the flow. The number of packets and bytes transferred alone can give clues as to whether that flow contains a file. If the number of bytes is too small or the packets too few, the possibility of that flow containing files are little; on the contrary that may indicate activities such as login attempts. File names included in the flows can indicate what is being transferred.

The use of flow index can greatly increase the efficiency when gathering the packets from the database to extract files. It eliminates the need to analyze each packet individually. Instead, all the packets from the flow can be obtained at once and analyzed together. Knowing which packets belong together greatly shortens the time it takes to examine the packets for their purpose. The reconstructed files can also be referenced back to the flow index to keep a record of their properties, such as the source and destination it was transferred between.

In this architecture, the most important stage is the real-time flow aggregation and extraction of properties to the index database. The more information able to be obtained from the flows the more complete the index would be, and in turn, gathering of packets and reconstructing them becomes more efficient. Two open source tools were tested for their functionalities and speed in flow aggregation.

4 SIMULATION AND RESULTS

4.1 Aguri2

Aguri2 is the primary aggregation tool for agurim, a multi-dimensional flow aggregation tool [10]. It produces aggregated flow records using the pcap library, and can achieve near real-time capture and aggregation of flow data. While capturing flow data, users can set custom intervals to which the flow data are written to a log file. Each log file contains aggregated flow summary of flows captured within that interval. The log files include source and destination IP addresses, source and destination ports, number of bytes transferred, and number of packets. Agurim can then be used on these log files to further aggregate them.

Aguir2 can be configured to customize the types of packets aggregated into each flow by using the wild card option. This provides more flexibility in the outcome. For this simulation, the default option was selected, with the interval set to 10 seconds. A log file was created every 10 seconds and saved to a directory, agurim was then configured to aggregate all the log file dataset from that directory. The aggregation of flow data was fast, and by setting the interval to 10 seconds, the final aggregated results were updated every 10 seconds, creating a near real-time

outcome. However, Aguri2 was not able to obtain many of the properties this architecture wanted, such as duration of the flow, and the start and end time.

4.2 Nfdump

The second tool tested for flow aggregation was the open source netflow processing tool Nfdump. Nfdump can process both captured pcap files, as well as netflow data. The performance of Nfdump was tested on an available pcap file first. Netflow data was first extracted from the pcap file using nfpcapd. Nfdump was then used on the netflow files generated and saved to an output file.

The pcap file was 57.3 MB, and the netflow data extracted from it was 407.1kb. Nfdump was able to process the netflow data and save the properties information at a rate of 294000 flows/second, taking less than 0.03 seconds to process all the netflow data obtained from the test pcap file. Furthermore, nfdump is very flexible and is capable of extracting a large variety of flow information and saving them in different formats—an advantage when constructing the flow index database.

Some of the information nfdump can obtain include source and destination IP addresses and ports, start and end time of flow, duration of flow, protocol used, number of packets, and number of bytes transferred. This satisfies the information needed in the proposed architecture except for the file names. The fast processing speed achieved by nfdump is in part due to it only analyzing netflow data, and to find file names, it would have to examine more than that, sacrificing some of its efficiency.

For nfdump, netflow data is collected using the nfcapd tool, which by default, stores netflow data in files every five minutes. Nfdump then reads and aggregates all these files into the output flow data. Similar to Aguri2, nfdump can also customize the intervals in which captured netflow data are stored, achieving near real-time flow aggregation.

5 CONCLUSIONS AND FUTURE WORK

This paper proposes a new architecture targeted at efficient file extraction from network traffic. As analyzing each packet to determine whether it contains a file is too resource and time consuming, a flow index is constructed with the properties of the network flows. The flow index is used to enable fast collection of corresponding packets, where files can then be reconstructed.

Two tools, Aguri2 and nfdump, were used to test for real-time flow aggregation and feature extraction. Neither of these tools were capable of extracting file names within the flows. Between the two tools, nfdump can obtain more flow features than Aguri2. However Aguri2 is more flexible in the fact that it can customize how flows are aggregated. Nfdump aggregates flows according to source and destination IP and ports, meaning packets with the same source and destination IP/ports are saved as the same flow. Neither of these two tools are completely real-time, though it is possible to accomplish near real-time by shortening the intervals for each captured flow record. This could be done by periodically re-aggregating all the flow data generated and updating the flow index. For the proposed architecture, flow information is saved to the index database when that flow ends, saving computing resources and preventing the flow index from containing partial flow information.

For future work, other tools can be tested for real-time flow aggregation and feature extraction, especially for file names and all the necessary flow information. Furthermore, research would be done into the computing and time efficiency in having a second machine which takes the packets in the database, process them and saves all packets according to flow. This means having them in the correct order and discarding redundant packets. This way, once the flow index references the database, the target packets are located together, providing faster collection of packets. Furthermore, although this paper focuses mainly on the technical aspects of aggregating evidence through network traffic, the legal issues surrounding the obtaining of those traffic also need to be put into perspective.

In conclusion, because of the limit of current computing power and the large amount of network traffic, it is quite impossible to extract all files from network traffic in real-time, even though it would provide investigators with a huge advantage and an extra source of evidence. However, with the architecture proposed in this paper, this process can be efficiently accomplished with available resources.

REFERENCES

[1] T. J. Holt, A. M. Bossler, and K. C. Seigfried-Spellar. 2015. *Cybercrime and digital forensics: An introduction*. Routledge, New York, NY.
[2] E. S. Pilli, R. C. Joshi, and R. Niyogi. 2010. Network forensic frameworks: Survey and research challenges. *Digital Investigation*, 7(1), 14-27.
[3] S. Davidoff and J. Ham. 2012. *Network forensics tracking hackers through cyberspace*. Prentice Hall, Upper Saddle River, NJ.
[4] R. Tian, L. Batten, R. Islam, and S. Versteeg. 2009. An automated classification system based on the strings of trojan and virus families. *Malicious and Unwanted Software (MALWARE), 2009 4th International Conference on*, 23-30.
[5] S. Sen, O. Spatscheck, and D. Wang. Accurate scalable in network identification of p2p traffic using application signatures. In *Proc. of 13th international conference on WWW*, pp. 512-521.
[6] Yiming Gong. 2005. Identifying P2P Users Using Traffic Analysis. (July, 2005). Retrieved May 1, 2017 https://www.symantec.com/connect/articles/identifying-p2p-users-using-traffic-analysis.
[7] T. Karagiannis, K. Papagiannaki, and M. Faloutsos. 2005. Blinc: Multilevel traffic classification in the dark. In *Proc. ACM SIGCOMM*, pp. 229-240.
[8] D. Wang, T. Li, S. Liu, J. Zhang, and C. Liu. 2007. Dynamical Network Forensics Based on Immune Agent. *Natural Computation, 2007. ICNC 2007. Third International Conference on*, 3, 651-656.
[9] A. Moore, J. Hall, C. Kreibich, E. Harris, and I. Pratt. Architecture of a Network Monitor. In PAM, 2003.
[10] "aguri2" 2012, https://github.com/necoma/aguri2.

Information Privacy of Cyber Transportation System: Opportunities and Challenges

Meng Han*
Kennesaw State University
1100 South Marietta Pkwy
Marietta, GA 30060
menghan@kennesaw.edu

Lei Li
Kennesaw State University
1100 South Marietta Pkwy
Marietta, GA 30060
lli13@kennesaw.edu

Xiaoqing Peng
Central South University
932 Lushan S Rd
Changsha, China 410078
xqpeng@csu.edu.cn

Zhen Hong
Zhejiang Sci-Tech University
Georgia Institute of Technology
Atlanta, GA 30332
zhong@zstu.edu.cn

Mohan Li
Jinan University
206 Qianshan Road
Zhuhai, China
limohan@jnu.edu.cn

ABSTRACT

The Cyber Transport Systems (CTSs) have made significant advancement along with the development of the information technology and transportation industries worldwide. The rapid proliferation of cyber transportation technology provides rich information and infinite possibilities for our society to understand and use the complex inherent mechanism, which governs the novel intelligence world. In addition, applying information technology to cyber transportation applications open a range of new application scenarios, such as vehicular safety, energy efficiency, reduced pollution, and intelligent maintenance services. However, while enjoying the services and convenience provided by CTS, users, vehicles, even the systems might lose privacy during information transmitting and processing. This paper summarizes the state-of-art research findings on information privacy issues in a broad range. We firstly introduce the typical types of information, and the basic mechanisms of information communication in CTS. Secondly, considering the information privacy issues of CTS, we present the literature on information privacy issues and privacy protection approaches in CTS. Thirdly, we discuss the emerging challenges and the opportunities for the information technology community in CTS.

KEYWORDS

Information Privacy, Transportation, Cybersecurity, Survey

---

*Dr. Han is the corresponding author.

RIIT'17, Oct. 4-7, 2017, Rochester, NY, USA
© 2017 Association for Computing Machinery.
ACM ISBN 978-1-4503-5120-1/17/10...$15.00
https://doi.org/10.1145/3125649.3125652

ACM Reference format:
Meng Han, Lei Li, Xiaoqing Peng, Zhen Hong, and Mohan Li. 2017. Information Privacy of Cyber Transportation System: Opportunities and Challenges. In *Proceedings of RIIT'17, Rochester, NY, USA, Oct. 4-7, 2017*, 6 pages.
https://doi.org/10.1145/3125649.3125652

1 INTRODUCTION

As an important component of Cyber Physical Systems (CPSs)[17], Cyber Transport Systems (CTSs also referred as "Intelligent transportation systems") integrate information, computation, networking, and physical processes into the transportation system. The research on CPS, the superset of CTS, has formally commenced since the National Science Foundation (NSF) awarded large amounts of funds to a project titled "Science of Integration for Cyber Physical Systems" in 2006. More than 300 research and development CPS projects covering the theories, methods, tools, platforms, *etc.* were launched with the support of NSF. Then, IBM proposed their "smart planet" as one strategic solution of CPS practice in 2009 [14]. In Europe, correspondingly, 658 million Euro were invested by the European Union in 2013 to support the "Smart Cyber Physical Systems" program, targeting at improving the quality and performance of the products and services with innovative embedded information communication technology components and systems [1]. All these programs indicate the huge potential and the development space of CPSs.

Transportation represents the movement of people, animals and goods from one location to another. All automotive, aviation and rail systems, which belong to transportation systems, are playing a crucial role in the communication and interaction of our society. The transportation system, formed by automotive, aviation, and rail systems with structural components, has a direct impact on the nations productivity, environment, and energy consumption. As shown in Fig.1, modes, elements, and functions are three main components of transportation. All infrastructure, vehicles, and operation provide freight and passenger the movement by air, rail, road, and water, *etc.* In a typical CPS, physical components and

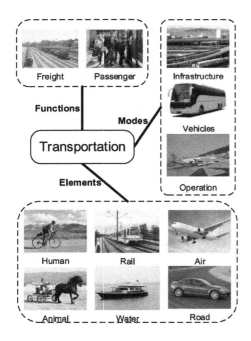

Figure 1: Elements and Functions of Transportation.

information involved are controlled or monitored continuously by discrete computing. A cyber transport system just provides such ample supply of examples of CPSs, considering all automotive, aviation and rail systems are controlled and monitored by corresponding communications and computations. Therefore, a CTS becomes one of the most important CPSs to improve our society's efficiency, safety, and stability.

Along with the development of CTSs, bounteous information is generated, transferred and analyzed within and without the system. All these data are shared and used progressively in applications such as collision avoidance, intelligent traffic control, health care monitoring, and even self-driving vehicles. However, while users are enjoying the convenience and functions brought by CTS, the security and privacy issues become important fundamental challenges on the aspect of usability and safety. Trains, subways, vehicles, and traffic lights are all managed and monitored by some CTSs. That means an electronic intruder potentially could affect vehicle speeds or even cause a horrible collision. It is also conceivable that adversaries or hackers could break the whole traffic in a major city and cause big chaos by attempting to simultaneously control all the traffic lights to red or to green. With the development of more and more complex CTSs, opportunities and challenges regarding the privacy issues in CTSs are emerging simultaneously. The security & privacy issues of CTSs are attracting more and more attentions from both industry and academia. Up to now, NSF in 2016 continued its commitment to securing cyberspace by awarding $74.5 million in research grants through the NSF Secure and Trustworthy Cyberspace (SaTC) program.

As far as we know, unfortunately, quite a few works make a comprehensive expounding and analysis for the privacy issues in CTSs. Considering the road safety, traffic management, and driver convenience, the work in [13] summarized the security and privacy issues of smart vehicles equipped with the recording, processing, positioning, and location devices. This work only considers the very earlier stage of CTSs, and many advanced techniques were not considered. Considering the message privacy problems in vehicle-to-vehicle communications, Wu *et al.* [21] tried to balance safety, privacy, and trustworthiness. Although the concern of privacy is acknowledged in [21], it is still a communication-oriented research. Most recently, Xiong *et al.* [22] surveyed the intelligent transportation of CPSs and CPSSs (cyber physical social systems) addressing the characteristics, applications, constraints and challenges [12]. They incorporated the social features into traditional CTSs and pointed out several potential research directions. But the work in [22] focuses on the social feature [11], not the information privacy issues.

In this paper, we focus on the latest problems and techniques regarding the privacy issues in CTSs. We not only provide a comprehensive analysis from the aspect of information technology, but also in an interdisciplinary way illustrate the various aspects of information privacy issues in CTSs. Firstly, we give the bird's eye view of the development of CTSs and some examples of the typical problems as an introduction in Section 1. Secondly, some preliminary knowledge regarding CTSs along with the fundamental concepts and CTS architecture are presented in Section 2. Thirdly, in Section 3, we introduce the general privacy problems and the progress in traditional CPSs, and the emerging privacy issues in CTSs. Afterward, we illustrate the most typical privacy goal in CTSs. Then by introducing the features and applicability of different models, we summarize the up-to-date literatures in Section 4. Then, we point out some new challenges and opportunities in this new digital era, and propose a taxonomy which summarizes the state-of-arts. We also put forward some guidelines and possible solutions with respect to the privacy issues in CTSs. Finally, Section 5 concludes this paper.

2 PRELIMINARIES

In this section, we first introduce the basic concept of CPS and CTS. Then we construe the typical architecture of a CTS and the corresponding terminologies.

2.1 Cyber Physical Systems

A CPS generally represents a physical and engineered system in which the embedded operations are monitored, coordinated, and controlled by a computation and communication center. Similar to the Internet, which transforms interaction and communication among humans through information, a CPS attempts to transform the interaction and control the physical world around us through information.

A CPS brings the discrete and powerful logic of computing to the communication and control of the dynamics of physical and engineered systems. The control part of a CPS is a predominantly continuous-time system modeled by means of algebraic or trajectories. The communication part is predominantly an interaction system connecting the physical devices, information platform, and participating users. Computation is an essential part of a discrete-event system. As well as the further development, potentialities and challenges of CPSs are proliferating.

2.2 Cyber Transportation Systems

We consider the physical systems like automotive, aviation, and rail systems involving communication, computation, control, and physical devices as Cyber Transportation Systems (CTSs). As an indispensable category of CPSs, a CTS focuses on monitoring, control, and coordination of all kinds of transportation along with their information. As shown in Fig.2, information, as the core of a CTS, is the platform and materials for communication, computation, and control. Consistently, application, cyber space, and physical space together construct a CTS. The cyber space is a notional environment in which communications over computer networks occur, and the physical expanse considers the substantial existence in the real world. In this paper, we are going to pay special attention to the most conventional transportation on land, while other varieties of transportation can follow the similar techniques.

2.2.1 Infrastructure of a CTS. All infrastructures such as automotive, aviation, and rail systems could be considered as the foundation of CTSs. These physical existences of transportation provide a broad range of infrastructure to support CTSs. Specifically, from land, air to water, different kinds of cars, trains, planes, and watercraft construct the motions of transportation. Roads, bridges, parking places, kinds of stations, airports, and shipyards provide the immobilized support and sustentation to all kinds of motions. The interaction

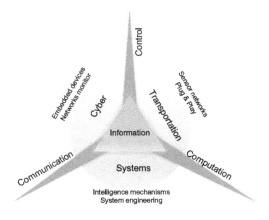

Figure 2: Three main parts of a CTS: communication, computation, and control.

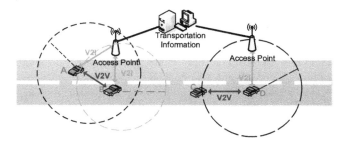

Figure 3: Three entities in a CTS: the Transportation Control Platform (TCP), the On-Board Units (OBUs) equipped on vehicles and the Road-Side Units (RSUs) including the access points.

between the mobile and immobile are the infrastructure of cyber networks. Video detectors, microwave detectors, radar detectors, and magneto detectors make the monitor, control, and communication happen within a CTS. Multiple sensors employed in roads, bridges, and fix decks further enhance the system's dexterity in transportation.

In a CTS, there are three entities to support control, communication, and computation:

(1) On-Board Units (OBUs) are devices installed in a vehicle, they allow the built-in system to collect data through identification of the vehicle and process the collected data which are stored in the OBU's memory. **(2)Road-Side Units (RSUs)** are infrastructure nodes with fixed base stations deployed along roadsides with the goal of increasing the overall coverage of a vehicular network. **(3)Transportation Control Platform (TCP)** actually is a supporting system for both OBUs and RSUs, as shown in Fig.3. During the communication process, data and information are collected and transferred over the TCP.

2.2.2 Communications in a CTS. The development of wireless networks is presumptuous to the progress of transportation systems. WAVE/802.11p and ZipBee/802.15.4 are two very typical communication protocols for data collection and transportation because of their improved competencies of data exchange among high-speed vehicles and between the vehicles and roadside infrastructure.

Traditionally, there are two types of CTS communications: Vehicle-to-Vehicle (**V2V**) communication and Vehicle-to-Infrastructure (**V2I**) communication. Recently, more mobile devices are installed in vehicles or carried in specific devices by the driver. We name the third type of communication as Device-to-Device (**D2D**) communication. Different from V2V and V2I, D2D is a multi-dimension channel, which not only provides simple information exchange but also supports the interaction of images, sounds, and GPS locations. As shown in Fig.4, besides V2I and V2V, D2D communication emerges because of the popularization of many kinds of mobile devices (mobile phones, wearable devices).

2.2.3 Computation in a CTS. Once observed and assimilated data is sent back to the control unit, computations are necessary to direct transportation. Customarily, there are two types of computations, one carried out on-line by remote devices or stations such as traffic lights and GPS assistants, while another is much more complicated and proficient in a data collecting center or central control board such as city traffic control center, airport terminal, *etc*. As shown in Fig.4, D2D communication and the CTS computation are intimately related. Manufactures and smart device servers provide computation support with D2D communication.

2.2.4 Applications of CTSs. Applications of CTSs could be divided into three categories in view of the real-time, resource cost, and computation usage: vehicle oriented CPS applications, vehicle-infrastructure CPS applications, and infrastructure oriented CPS applications.

3 PRIVACY ISSUES
3.1 General Privacy Issues in CPSs
Addressing the privacy requirements in CPSs, the works in [3] and [2] present the relative practical frameworks for assessing security risks in CPSs. When information is less than perfect, their frameworks could be used to benchmark the security risks.

The works in [20] discuss the limitations of the prevailing automotive CPSs. They particularly propose the privacy issue of geo-reference data. Although they point out the research directions regarding how to structure data collection and communication in a privacy preserving environment, this issue has not been well investigated till now.

Recently, the work in [4] explores the solutions for the design of CPSs through three aspects: models, abstractions,

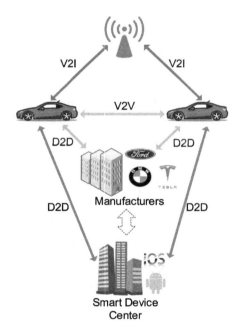

Figure 4: V2V, V2I, and D2D in CTSs.

and architectures. The authors point out that the challenges in large scale CPS applications can be solved by a combination of different disciplines.

3.2 Emerging Privacy Issues in CTSs
Considering the mobility, dynamic, and complexity of CTSs, many privacy issues in CTSs are emerging. We summarize the most typical concerns and problems addressed in the latest literatures in the following.

The work in [25] is the first one to study the privacy-preserving traffic volume measurement covering more than two locations instead of only one location in previous literatures. Zhou *et. al.* [24] designed a threshold credit based incentive mechanism for cloud-based vehicular. However, even though the intermediate nodes will receive rewards, they still have bottlenecks, and the credit cannot satisfy them.

Based on signatures, which could provide the basic message integrity, authentication and non-repudiation, the first category of privacy protection mechanisms are developed as follows. The authors of [18], also in [19], provided a detailed threat analysis and devised an appropriate security architecture. However, this category of techniques suffers from the burden of a heavy certificate management and optimization problem. The generation, delivery, storage and verification of certificates for all the keys result in unaffordable pressure to CTSs.

To mitigate the heavy overhead of signature management, the second category of mechanism is developed with the help of group signatures. A novel group signature based security framework is proposed in [8], which relies on temper-resistant devices for stopping adversarial attacks on CTSs.

Some other privacy preserving methods try to use a identity based cryptography strategy [16]. A recognizable identity is used by an entity as its public key and a trusted authority will use a master secret to generate a private key for each agent. With replaced pseudonyms for the identity of an entity, privacy is preserved. To achieve unsinkable privacy, in [23], an ideal device, which does not allow any attacker to extract any stored data, is proposed. But the assumption is too strong to be applied in practice. Even the assumption could be established, as shown in [15], an attacher could still collect substantial information to launch the side-channel attacks.

Drawing lessons from the aforementioned methods, the one-time identity-based aggregate signature [5] is proposed. The application of information-theoretic measures to anomaly detection is also studied [5, 6]. In [7], the authors assumed that the simplest explanation of some inconsistency in the received information has the highest probability to be correct, then they proposed a method that could handle both detection and correction of malicious data.

3.3 Privacy Goals in CTSs
In this section, we summarize the following seven privacy goals to be considered in CTS design and development. These privacy goals are general outlines for privacy concerns in CTSs, but it is not required to satisfy every goal in a single

application. Actually, some of the privacy goals are regarded as inter-constraint measures. **(1) Identity:** The identity of a vehicle should be protected. It is required that a vehicle should not be traced without all trusted authorities agreeing to disclose their identities, and the trajectory privacy of vehicles should also be ensured. **(2) Authentication:** Authentication represents the privacy protection against impersonation or adversary attacks. Messages in a CTS should be generated only by the authenticated senders no matter the messages are sent by RSUs or OBUs. **(3) Anonymity:** Identified entities would result in the loss of vehicles' privacy. If a message originator cannot be identified by communication monitoring, the anonymity goal is achieved. The lack of anonymity would result in serious privacy disclosure. **(4) Traceability:** Anonymity might be utilized by vehicles or other instances to release messages without the worry of being tracked. The authority should allow the identification of a vehicle if necessary. **(5) Revocability:** Similar to traceability, revocability represents the feature that an originator and the endorsers of any hazardous message could be identified. **(6) Scalability:** Scalability represents that a system is scalable and can host different levels of data access and workload. Take monitoring as an example, the privacy should be preserved no matter how many vehicles are being monitored in a system. **(7) Robustness:** In a dynamic CTS, robustness requires a system to allow the joining and leaving of any number of vehicles, and the privacy could be kept during the whole process.

4 CHALLENGES AND DIRECTIONS
4.1 Challenges of the Privacy in CTSs
Private information related to any data emitted, collected, or stored should be considered in CTSs.

4.1.1 Personal Identifiable Information.
A pivotal concept in privacy analysis is Personal Identifiable Information (PII). PII is any information that can be used to distinguish or trace an individual's identity. Therefore, a CTS needs to determine the extent to which the system will collect or store PII and PII-related information.

4.1.2 Communication Privacy in CTSs.
Communication privacy plays a very important role in CTS privacy since considerable data is commonly transmitted from vehicles, infrastructures or some other terminal devices. The communication process becomes extremely important to protect the privacy of sensitive information. However, the trusted authorization is hard to develop considering our requirement to use identity to guarantee integrity.

4.1.3 Location Privacy in CTSs.
Localization and tracking techniques enable accurate location estimation and tracking of vehicles in CTSs. Benefit of the advanced location identification, the information that whether a vehicle's location history congruously accessible, the privacy of a user and a vehicle confront a new privacy challenge [9, 10]. How to protect location privacy not only from the V2V and V2I communications but also from the D2D communications becomes an emerging challenge.

4.2 Future Directions and Opportunities
A CTS only has two information sources: Transportation networks and CPSs. With the development of smart phones and wearable devices, online social networks emerge as the third information source and this source has taken effect in the integration of a whole CTS.

4.2.1 Communication Privacy in CTSs.
Generally, there are two research directions with respect to communication privacy problems in CTSs. The first one is related to V2I communications, and two central concerns need to be addressed, namely: (1) the privacy of all participating vehicles should be preserved as well as the sensitive information in RSUs; (2) the communication with infrastructure might result in a large-scale vehicular network, which requires that a privacy protection scheme works efficiently in order to process big data. Without comprehensive information about the environment changes for drivers, the emerging problems *e.g.*, highway accidents and traffic jams are still hard to be well solved. Therefore, how to unambiguously accumulate real-time information regarding the driving status of numerous vehicles and the corresponding spatio-temporal occupations on the road in CTSs is still a very challenging issue.

4.2.2 Social Based Privacy in CTSs.
With the emerging of social networks, social media, and social applications, humans are connected and it is much easier to share and get useful information than ever before. Thus, a CTS has an increasing influence over individual's travel decisions and behaviors. However, CTSs generally do not quantitatively estimate the impacts from humans, organizations, and societies, which are uncertain, diverse, and complex [22]. The development of the social scenario is still not sufficient to address the many emerging challenges especially the privacy issues in CTSs. The social based privacy in CTSs involves the right of mandating personal privacy concerning storing, re-purposing, provision to third parties, and displaying of information pertaining to oneself via the CTS and internet. Therefore, social based privacy in CTSs is a broad direction for future study.

4.2.3 The Evaluation of CTS Privacy.
The evaluation metrics are also open problems in CTSs. Differential privacy, borrowed from the database field, aims to provide means to maximize the accuracy of query results while minimizing the chances of identifying privacy has been investigated for several years in data privacy. However, the limitation of differential privacy is apparent: (1) Differential privacy guarantees that the results of queries on two adjacent query pools cannot be distinguished very well. (2) An important consequence of differential privacy is that composing a differentially private function with any other function that does not depend on the database yields a function that is again differentially private. However, this is not easy to be guaranteed either.

The correlation of many different queries could provide a very high probability to de-anonymize the sensitive information.

4.2.4 More Other Potential Research Directions.
Besides all the aforementioned directions, there are more potential research directions due to the complexity, dynamics, and uncertainty of CTSs. **(1)Complexity and Dimensionality Protection**: Scaling to the full complexity and dimensionality of transportation data is an acute necessity in order to protect the privacy of information in CTSs. Research in this area requests a comprehensive understanding of the mechanism and deep insight of privacy issues in CTSs. So far, there is still no comprehensive research which considers the complexity and dimensionality in CTSs yet. **(2)Verification Architectures of Large-scale Data**: The architecture design is always a massive issue, but the below mentioned solution would resolve the issue fundamentally. Rather than verifying each new transportation system from scratch, developing domain specific verification frameworks to speed up the verification process with good scalability properties for the industrial setting would be a very valuable topic in the near future. **(3)Probabilistic Effects in CTSs**: Taking the probability distribution of the corresponding CTSs into account for the automatic stochastic message communication would be another potential research direction. The likelihood of a certain event would create many novel models to analyze the privacy and information transmitting. All these new models could also provide many research opportunities in the next several years.

5 CONCLUSION

In this paper, we summarize the up-to-date privacy issues in CTSs. We introduce the pivotal concepts and the architecture of a typical CTS. Overall, the development of reliable cyber transportation innovations and products will continue for a very long time. The privacy issues of the information in all these systems could be more and more important. The debate between privacy attacks and defense schemes will last extensively. There are still many opportunities to go alongside the challenges.

REFERENCES

[1] HORIZON 2020. 2015. Smart Cyber-Physical Systems. (2015). https://ec.europa.eu/programmes/horizon2020/en/h2020-section/smart-cyber-physical-systems
[2] Saurabh Amin, Galina A Schwartz, and Alefiya Hussain. 2013. In quest of benchmarking security risks to cyber-physical systems. IEEE Network 27, 1 (2013), 19–24. https://doi.org/10.1109/MNET.2013.6423187
[3] Saurabh Amin, Galina A. Schwartz, and S. Shankar Sastry. 2013. Security of interdependent and identical networked control systems. Automatica 49, 1 (2013), 186 – 192. https://doi.org/10.1016/j.automatica.2012.09.007
[4] Bharathan Balaji, Mohammad Abdullah Al Faruque, Nikil Dutt, Rajesh Gupta, and Yuvraj Agarwal. 2015. Models, Abstractions, and Architectures: The Missing Links in Cyber-physical Systems. (2015), 82 pages.
[5] E Earl Eiland and Lorie M Liebrock. 2006. An application of information theory to intrusion detection. In Information Assurance, 2006. IWIA 2006. Fourth IEEE International Workshop on. IEEE, 16–pp.
[6] Laura Feinstein, Dan Schnackenberg, Ravindra Balupari, and Darrell Kindred. 2003. Statistical approaches to DDoS attack detection and response. In DARPA Information Survivability Conference and Exposition, 2003. Proceedings, Vol. 1. IEEE, 303–314.
[7] Philippe Golle, Dan Greene, and Jessica Staddon. 2004. Detecting and correcting malicious data in VANETs. In Proceedings of the 1st ACM international workshop on Vehicular ad hoc networks. ACM, 29–37.
[8] Jinhua Guo, John P Baugh, and Shengquan Wang. 2007. A group signature based secure and privacy-preserving vehicular communication framework. In 2007 Mobile Networking for Vehicular Environments. IEEE, 103–108.
[9] Meng Han, Qilong Han, Lijie Li, Ji Li, and Yingshu Li. 2017. Maximizing influence in sensed heterogenous social network with privacy preservation. International Journal of Sensor Networks (2017), 1–11.
[10] Meng Han, Ji Li, Zhipeng Cai, and Qilong Han. 2016. Privacy reserved influence maximization in gps-enabled cyber-physical and online social networks. In 2016 IEEE International Conferences on Social Computing and Networking (SocialCom). IEEE, 284–292.
[11] Meng Han, Mingyuan Yan, Zhipeng Cai, and Yingshu Li. 2016. An exploration of broader influence maximization in timeliness networks with opportunistic selection. Journal of Network and Computer Applications 63 (2016), 39–49.
[12] Meng Han, Mingyuan Yan, Zhipeng Cai, Yingshu Li, Xingquan Cai, and Jiguo Yu. 2017. Influence maximization by probing partial communities in dynamic online social networks. Transactions on Emerging Telecommunications Technologies 28, 4 (2017).
[13] Jean-Pierre Hubaux, Srdjan Capkun, and Jun Luo. 2004. The security and privacy of smart vehicles. IEEE Security & Privacy Magazine 2, LCA-ARTICLE-2004-007 (2004), 49–55.
[14] IBM. 2007. IBM builds a smarter planet. (2007). http://www.ibm.com/smarterplanet/us/en/
[15] Eike Kiltz and Krzysztof Pietrzak. 2010. Leakage resilient elgamal encryption. In International Conference on the Theory and Application of Cryptology and Information Security. Springer, 595–612.
[16] Jie Li, Huang Lu, and Mohsen Guizani. 2015. ACPN: a novel authentication framework with conditional privacy-preservation and non-repudiation for VANETs. IEEE Transactions on Parallel and Distributed Systems 26, 4 (2015), 938–948.
[17] Asare Philip, Broman David, Lee Edward A., Prinsloo Gerro, Torngren Martin, and Sunder S. Shyam. 2012. Cyber-Physical Systems. (2012). http://cyberphysicalsystems.org/
[18] Maxim Raya and Jean Pierre Hubaux. 2005. The Security of Vehicular Ad Hoc Networks. (2005), 11–12.
[19] Maxim Raya and Jean-Pierre Hubaux. 2007. Securing vehicular ad hoc networks. Journal of Computer Security 15, 1 (2007), 39–68.
[20] Daniel B Work and Alexandre M Bayen. 2008. Impacts of the mobile internet on transportation cyberphysical systems: traffic monitoring using smartphones. (2008), 18–20 pages.
[21] Q. Wu, J. Domingo-Ferrer, and Gonzalez-Nicolas. 2010. Balanced Trustworthiness, Safety, and Privacy in Vehicle-to-Vehicle Communications. IEEE Transactions on Vehicular Technology 59, 2 (2010), 559–573. https://doi.org/10.1109/TVT.2009.2034669
[22] Gang Xiong, Fenghua Zhu, Xiwei Liu, Xisong Dong, Wuling Huang, Songhang Chen, and Kai Zhao. 2015. Cyber-physical-social system in intelligent transportation. IEEE/CAA Journal of Automatica Sinica 2, 3 (2015), 320–333. https://doi.org/10.1109/JAS.2015.7152667
[23] Chenxi Zhang, Rongxing Lu, Xiaodong Lin, P-H Ho, and Xuemin Shen. 2008. An efficient identity-based batch verification scheme for vehicular sensor networks. In INFOCOM 2008. The 27th Conference on Computer Communications. 246–250.
[24] Jun Zhou, Xiaolei Dong, Zhenfu Cao, and Athanasios V Vasilakos. 2015. Secure and Privacy Preserving Protocol for Cloud-Based Vehicular DTNs. IEEE Transactions on Information Forensics and Security 10, 6 (2015), 1299–1314. https://doi.org/10.1109/TIFS.2015.2407326
[25] Yian Zhou, Shigang Chen, You Zhou, Min Chen, and Qingjun Xiao. Privacy-Preserving Multi-Point Traffic Volume Measurement Through Vehicle-to-Infrastructure Communications. IEEE Transactions on Vehicular Technology 64, 12 (????), 5619–5630.

Monitoring Multicopters Energy Consumption

Ilenia Fronza
Free University of Bozen-Bolzano
Piazza Domenicani 3
Bolzano, Italy 39100
ilenia.fronza@unibz.it

Nabil El Ioini
Free University of Bozen-Bolzano
Piazza Domenicani 3
Bolzano, Italy 39100
nabil.elioini@unibz.it

Luis Corral
ITESM / UAQ
E. Gonzalez 500
Queretaro, Mexico 76130
lrcorralv@itesm.mx

Matthias Moroder
FlyingBasket
Via Scurcia 54
Ortisei (BZ), Italy 39046
matthias.moroder@flyingbasket.it

Moritz Moroder
FlyingBasket
Via Scurcia 54
Ortisei (BZ), Italy 39046
moritz.moroder@flyingbasket.it

ABSTRACT

Multicopters are small, typically unmanned helicopters having more than two rotors. The wide range of possible applications of multicopters, spanning from environmental research to recreation, has raised the need to come up with innovative solutions to reduce the power demand of these platforms, with the goal of guaranteeing safe completion of missions. To this end, it is of paramount importance to understand the way in which the energy is invested and spent. The goal of this work is to provide reliable means to monitor multicopters energy consumption. We developed a monitoring platform to keep track of the energy consumption of multicopters. The platform relies on a set of sensors to collect the energy consumption data at different points of interest; data are then visualized in a monitoring dashboard. The monitoring system allows further analysis of the recorded data, which could be used to optimize multicopters energy consumption.

CCS CONCEPTS

•Software and its engineering → Software creation and management;

KEYWORDS

Multicopters, drones, energy consumption, monitoring

ACM Reference format:
Ilenia Fronza, Nabil El Ioini, Luis Corral, Matthias Moroder, and Moritz Moroder. 2017. Monitoring Multicopters Energy Consumption. In *Proceedings of RIIT'17, Rochester, NY, USA, October 4–7, 2017*, 6 pages.
DOI: 10.1145/3125649.3125657

1 INTRODUCTION

Multicopters are small, typically unmanned helicopters having more than two rotors. Multicopters come in many configurations: the names tricopter, quadcopter, hexacopter and octocopter are frequently used to refer to 3-, 4-, 6- and 8-rotor helicopters, respectively.

Multicopters have experienced a fast diffusion in the last few years, and many fields have explored the possibility to take advantage of multicopters technology. Therefore, the usage of multicopters can be encountered in many fields, such as climate science, energy and environmental research, surveillance, and hobby or recreation. This wide range of application purposes has brought a number of challenges and opportunities for different research paths that have been focusing on different aspects, such as applications, airworthiness, autonomy, and energy efficiency. In this regard, there is a need of strategies to promote efficient energy usage to reduce the power demand of these platforms, with the goal of guaranteeing safe completion of missions.

In the past, research has focused on energy efficient mobile targets (such as smartphones and wearables) [12]; however, limited effort has been spent in understanding how to improve the energy efficiency of multicopters. The proposed strategies adopt mainly two approaches, namely the optimization of hardware components or the development of built-in software that is specifically designed to optimize resources utilization. In both cases, having the ability to understand the way in which the energy is invested and spent is of paramount importance to propose effective solutions. This opens the doors to design, implement and validate reliable means to collect and analyze data about multicopters energy consumption.

In order to contribute to address this issue, we developed a monitoring platform to keep track of the energy consumption of multicopters. The platform relies on a set of sensors to collect energy consumption data at different points of interest, then a monitoring dashboards visualizes the data in a meaningful way [7, 8]. With the goal of collecting power consumption data, a monitoring board is built and equipped with sensors to monitor the multicopter motors, a voltage sensor, and a current sensor to monitor the total current draw.

Additionally, the monitoring board can be easily extended to support more sensors. All the sensors are connected to a micro controller, which runs the monitoring software. The monitoring system allows further analysis of the recorded data, which could be used to optimize the energy consumption of the multicopter.

The rest of the paper is organized as follows: Section 2 covers the related work on the optimization of energy consumption for non-stationary platforms; Section 3 describes the architecture of the proposed monitoring system; Section 4 provides the implementation details; Section 5 draws conclusions and sets possible directions for future work.

2 RELATED WORK

The areas of application for unmanned aerial vehicles span from simple entertainment to professional fields, which has caused a growing interest in having multicopters as research subject. As multicopters expand their ability to perform longer and even mission-critical tasks (for instance, delivery of medical aid), a main concern sets upon their performance is the trustworthiness during the execution of these tasks.

Trust and dependability can be defined from different standpoints, for instance the ability to perform accurately, safely and autonomously [13]. In that front, the autonomy of a multicopter depends highly on the energy that its power source (i.e., a battery) can provide, in conjunction with the weight, payload and other operational aspects of the multicopter itself. Cellular phones, tablets, wireless sensors, wearables, and multicopters are systems that rely on their battery capacity, which is as well one of the most important limitations to their operation. As a result, the potential usefulness of multicopters is impeded by the energy constraint. Therefore, there is a clear need to accomplish a more efficient battery usage to reduce the power demand of multicopters targets.

Strategies to reduce power usage can imply optimization and development of hardware components, or development of built-in software that is specifically designed to optimize the utilization of the resources at hand. Park et al. [11] identified the low volume of research works in energy aware techniques for multicopters, discussing that energy efficiency and battery aging affect the multicopter delivery business. Authors discuss that no prior work has extensively assessed the problem for energy awareness in the multicopter business. In their paper, they propose a holistic and detailed analysis on the profitability and time to delivery of the multicopter delivery business.

Clarke [1] outlines critical attributes for the airworthy operation of a multicopter. Even though almost all the characteristics concern the maneuverability, safety, and other airborne conditions of the multicopter, the author also mentions characteristics related to the resource usage of the device; for instance, providing "a sufficient source of power to maintain movement, to implement the controls, and to operate sensors and data feeds, for the duration of the flight and the ability to navigate to destination locations within the operational space".

In software-based approaches used for battery optimization in multicopters, to the best of our knowledge, there is currently no software solution available on the market which tries to optimize the battery consumption in such target platform as multicopters. Corral et al. present research works that exemplify methods to measure the energy consumed by multicopters [3] and to optimize energy consumption in multicopters using preset flight profiles [2].

Zorbas et al. [14] studied a mathematical formulation for minimizing the total energy consumption of a fleet of camera-enabled multicopters, depending on the localization and height of the event they should cover. Following their proposed algorithm, the authors claim savings up to 150% of the total energy consumed. Similarly, Di Franco and Buttazzo [6] propose an energy-aware path-planning algorithm that minimizes energy consumption while satisfying a set of other requirements, such as coverage and resolution.

The research works of Pace et al. [10], Huang et al. [9] and Da Silva et al. [5] also concern algorithms to plan missions in a way that the return home is guaranteed.

3 MONITORING SYSTEM ARCHITECTURE

As shown in Figure 1, the monitoring system proposed in this paper has two main components: the *Monitoring Board* and the *Ground Station*. The *Monitoring Board* is mounted on the muliticopter, while the *Ground Station* is next to the pilot on the ground. The remaining part of this section details the architecture of these two components.

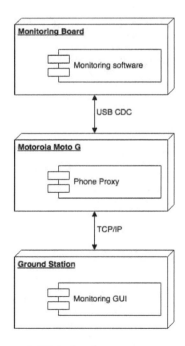

Figure 1: Main hardware components.

3.1 Monitoring Board

The architecture of the monitoring board can be illustrated as shown in Figure 2. The board is an integrated system that links a set of modules to a microcontroller that runs the monitoring software. The sensors are used as data acquisition modules, which are deployed at different points of interest to collect real-time power consumption information. A first module integrates the current sensors to monitor the power consumed by the multicopter motors. A second module of the monitoring board is equipped with a voltage sensor and a current sensor measuring the total current draw. The microcontroller primary function is to process and aggregate the collected data, then send it to the ground station using a transmitter module. The microcontroller needs to be updated when new sensors are deployed.

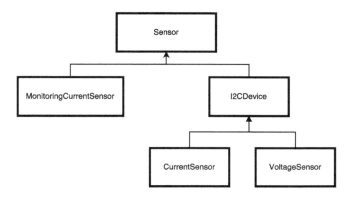

Figure 3: Class diagram of the Sensor library.

3.1.3 Transmitter module. The transmitter module handles the connection and the transmission of the collected data to the ground station. It uses different protocols including GSM/GPRS/EDGE, UMTS, HSPA+ and LTE to connect to the internet, then a Virtual Private Network (VPN) is used to establish a direct TCP connection with the ground station.

3.2 Ground Station

The ground station is the front-end of the monitoring system. It allows the visualization off all the collected data at different levels of granularity. The data shown on the ground station can represent single sensors data or an aggregation of sensors data. It can show real time data, and also data of previous flights.

4 IMPLEMENTATION

This section describes the hardware and software components and provides details about the technologies that have been adopted for their implementation.

4.1 Hardware Components

4.1.1 Multicopter. An in-house platform has been used, the so-called FB1-T, which is large enough to mount external sensors for measurements. As shown in Figure 4, the FB1-T is a X4 configuration (i.e., its arms form an X) and on each arm there is one motor, therefore 4 motors in total. Having a motor-to-motor distance of approximately 1.2 m and a weight of 23 kg, this platform solves all the problems related to added space and weight for monitoring hardware.

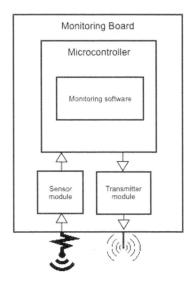

Figure 2: Monitoring board architecture.

3.1.1 Monitoring Software. The monitoring software is responsible of processing the collected data, which means synthesizing and aggregating data to provide different views on the multicopter power consumption. Data sources are:

- the different voltage and current sensors;
- the flight controller, which provides altitude, position, acceleration, radio control inputs and others.

To provide a modular architecture, all the software components are designed as a set of modules.

3.1.2 Sensor Module. The sensor module provides the following three classes used in the monitoring software: MonitoringCurrentSensor, CurrentSensor, and VoltageSensor. As shown in Figure 3, all classes are derived from the base class Sensor. The class Sensor provides the *update()* function, which can be used to trigger the data acquisition by the sensor.

The whole system is powered by a 1,4 kWh Lithium-Polymer battery, configured in 12S2P, meaning two times 12 cells in series afterwards paralleled together. Fully charged, the battery voltage under no load is 50,4 V. The multicopter flies thanks to 27" propellers paired with motors consuming up to 4 kW peak power. The motors are brushless, therefore they run on three-phase electric power, which is supplied by the Electronic Speed Controllers (ESCs). The A3 by DJI[1] is used as flight

---

[1]http://www.dji.com/a3/info

Figure 4: The multicopter used in this work to test the monitoring system.

controller, together with the Lightbridge 2 as radio control link[2].

4.1.2 Monitoring Board. The monitoring board has been built using a small but powerful microcontroller named Teensy 3.2[3]. The choice of this microcontroller was strictly based on its compatibility with the Arduino IDE. The microcontroller is connected to 8 hall effect current sensors of type "Allegro ACS758-200", which is a current sensor capable of bidirectional measurements up to 200A. The built-in analog to digital converter (ADC) of the Teensy 3.2 evaluates the output of the sensor, a signal between 0 and 3.3V depending on the current flowing though the sensor.

4.2 Software Components

4.2.1 Monitoring software. The goal of the monitoring software is to monitor and log the data given from various sources. It takes the analog input from up to 8 sensors and normalizes their values to Ampere. It receives input data from specific ports to gather the information from the flight controller, such as GPS position, orientation, accelerometer and gyroscope data, motor outputs. The monitoring software has been developed using the Arduino platform, as it simplifies the software development for Teensy using standard C, C++ as well as custom built libraries.

4.2.2 Ground Station app. The counterpart for the monitoring software is programmed using Qt, to allow cross-platform software deployment. It includes the GUI part of the system, which allows users to visualize the status and changes in energy consumption of the different components. It provides live view of the data sent from the phone on the drone through cellular network, and also allows to review the log files and to visualize the data stored. It shows voltage, current for up to 8 sensors on the monitoring board, total current and power consumption, which is also plotted. As the software is used

[2]http://www.dji.com/lightbridge-2/info
[3]https://www.pjrc.com/teensy/

to monitor the hybrid version of the multicopter too, the target voltage for the generator and the current from and to the generator and the batteries are also displayed separately. As the generator controller measures the temperature and RPM of the generator, these values can also be displayed, including a warning if the temperature increases.

Figure 6 shows a screenshot of the Ground Station app. On the left, there is a animated 3D reproduction of the aircraft's movements. In the center the voltage and total load current (blue) is shown. In the diagram below, the load power is plotted. On the top right the aircraft's horizontal movements are plotted on a map. On the center right the currents drawn by the motors are displayed. On the bottom right, the remote control stick inputs are shown.

4.2.3 Phone Proxy App. The Proxy App forwards the data from the Monitoring Board to the Ground Station. The Phone App has two threads running all the time. Thread 1 handles the communication with the Monitoring Board over USB, Thread 2 handles the communitation with the Ground Station over TCP.

Figure 5 shows the workflow of the two threads. Additionally, in order to forward the data to the Ground Station, the Proxy App also saves the all data received via USB to a file for later use.

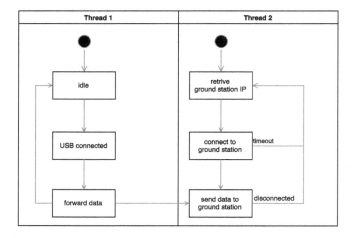

Figure 5: Flow diagram of the Proxy App.

4.3 Technologies

Qt[4], a cross-platform application framework that is used for developing application software that can be run on various software and hardware platforms with little or no change in the underlying codebase, while still being a native application with native capabilities and speed. Qt is currently being developed both by The Qt Company, a company listed on the Nasdaq Helsinki Stock Exchange and the Qt Project under open-source governance, involving individual developers and firms working to advance Qt. Qt is available with both

[4]https://www.qt.io

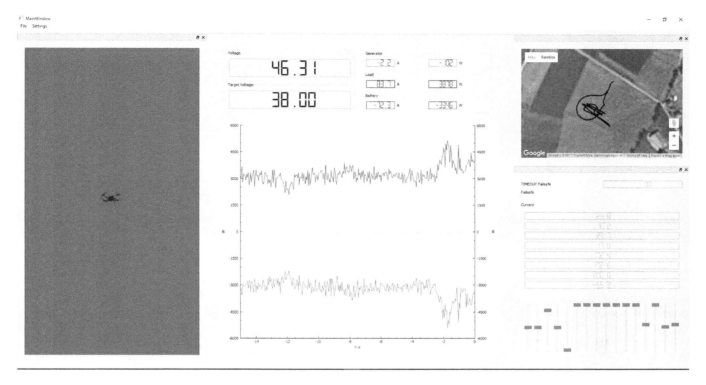

Figure 6: The Monitoring GUI running on the Ground Station.

commercial and open source GPL 2.0, GPL 3.0, and LGPL 3.0 licenses.

Arduino[5], a computer hardware and software company, project, and user community that designs and manufactures micro-controller kits for building digital devices and interactive objects that can sense and control objects in the physical world. Arduino boards are available commercially in pre-assembled form, or as do-it-yourself kits. The Arduino project provides the Arduino integrated development environment (IDE), which is a cross-platform application written in the programming language Java. It includes a code editor with many features, such as syntax highlighting, brace matching, cutting-pasting and searching-replacing text, and automatic indenting, and provides simple one-click mechanism to compile and upload programs to an Arduino board.

4.4 Initial System Evaluation

The system has been deployed on the multicopter platform FB1-T. System evaluation was divided in two phases. First, the sensors have been calibrated on the ground to verify the data correctness. Afterwards, the repeatability of the measurements has been evaluated by checking that similar results were collected by performing similar manoeuvres during different fights. Overall 25 flights were performed with a total flight time of 3 hours. The correctness of the current measurements was also confirmed by comparing them to the control data from the flight controller, which are also logged. The logs

[5]https://www.arduino.cc

confirm that requested changes in power lead to proportional changes in the measured consumption.

The collected data can be used for different purposes; for instance, they can support the improvement of maintenance cycles as problems with the motors or the frame of the multi-copter can be recognized. This was confirmed during testing, as there was a difference in power consumption by two diagonally opposed motors, as shown in Figure 7, caused by bearing problems and bad alignment of the motors. This finding was confirmed by the output signal of the flight controller, which changed proportionally to the measured current on each motor.

4.5 Scalability

The proposed solution could be implemented on different models of multicopters having the power cables of the motor controllers accessible. Adaptations could be needed for a multicopter with lower current requirements: the current sensors used in our application have a measurement accuracy of ±3% over a range of ±200A. More precise sensors are available for lower current ranges. Furthermore a smaller formfactor could also be achieved when using smaller sensors for lower currents. Other changes might include different sensors depending on the application.

5 CONCLUSION AND FUTURE WORK

The potential usefulness of multicopters in many mission critical applications (such as emergency relief and surveillance)

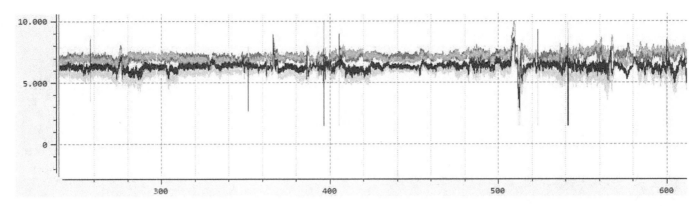

Figure 7: The difference in power of two diagonally opposed motors (M1 in red and M3 in green) compared to the other two opposing motors (M2 in yellow and M4 in blue).

is prevented by the battery life constrain. This limitation is increased when power resources are needed not only to fly successfully, but also to power on-board facilities such as a built-in videocamera. Therefore, energy usage needs to be optimized to guarantee safe completion of missions and, consequently, to take full advantage of multicopters in all the potential application domains. To this end, collecting and analysing data is a necessary step towards understanding how the energy is invested and how it can be used more efficiently.

In this paper, we presented a monitoring platform to keep track of multicopters energy consumption. The proposed system uses a set of sensors to collect the energy consumption data at different points of interest; then, the collected data is visualized in a dashboard that can show single sensors data or an aggregation of sensors data. Moreover, the dashboard allows to visualize both real time data and historical data.

The framework proposed in this paper collects relevant data from the multicopters during their flights. Further work is now needed to perform a large scale evaluation. Then, a next step in the research roadmap [4] is to use the data collected by our framework to develop tools and strategies that leverage this knowledge to optimise multicopters energy consumption. For example, the collected data can provide the basis to extend the duration of missions following different approaches, such as:

- modelling multicopter's energy consumption to find the energy consumption for different flight trajectories;
- for an automated flying multicopter, a model predicting energy consumption could be used to calculate the most energy efficient flight path, including speed and acceleration, in an environment with fixed obstacles;
- for manually piloted multicopters, a software could be implemented with a energy saving mode which modifies the pilot's remote control input to limit the energy consumption of the multicopter.

The monitoring board proposed in this paper can be easily extended to support more sensors and to collect further data about the multicopter's energy draining process.

REFERENCES

[1] Roger Clarke. 2014. Understanding the drone epidemic. *Computer Law & Security Review* 30, 3 (2014), 230–246.

[2] L. Corral, I. Fronza, N. El Ioini, and A. Ibershimi. 2016. A measurement tool to track drones battery consumption during flights. *Lecture Notes in Computer Science (including subseries Lecture Notes in Artificial Intelligence and Lecture Notes in Bioinformatics)* 9847 (2016), 334–344.

[3] L. Corral, I. Fronza, N. El Ioini, and A. Ibershimi. 2016. Towards optimization of energy consumption of drones with software-based flight analysis. In *Proceedings of the International Conference on Software Engineering and Knowledge Engineering, SEKE*. 543–546.

[4] Luis Corral, Ilenia Fronza, and Nabil El Ioini. 2017. The Incorporation of Drones as Object of Study in Energy-aware Software Engineering. In *Proceedings of the 19th International Conference on Enterprise Information Systems - Volume 2: ICEIS,*. INSTICC, ScitePress, 721–726.

[5] Rone Ilídio da Silva and Mario A Nascimento. 2016. On best drone tour plans for data collection in wireless sensor network. In *Proceedings of the 31st Annual ACM Symposium on Applied Computing*. ACM, 703–708.

[6] Carmelo Di Franco and Giorgio Buttazzo. 2015. Energy-aware coverage path planning of UAVs. In *Autonomous Robot Systems and Competitions (ICARSC), 2015 IEEE International Conference on*. IEEE, 111–117.

[7] Stephen Few. 2013. *Information Dashboard Design: Displaying data for at-a-glance monitoring*. Analytics Press.

[8] I. Fronza, A. Janes, A. Sillitti, G. Succi, and S. Trebeschi. 2013. Cooperation wordle using pre-attentive processing techniques. *2013 6th International Workshop on Cooperative and Human Aspects of Software Engineering, CHASE 2013 - Proceedings* (2013), 57–64.

[9] Yu-Te Huang, Yao-Hua Ho, Hao-hua Chu, and Ling-Jyh Chen. 2015. Adaptive Drone Sensing with Always Return-To-Home Guaranteed. In *Proceedings of the 1st International Workshop on Experiences with the Design and Implementation of Smart Objects*. ACM, 7–12.

[10] Pasquale Pace, Gianluca Aloi, Giuseppe Caliciuri, and Giancarlo Fortino. 2015. Management and coordination framework for aerial-terrestrial smart drone networks. In *Proceedings of the 1st International Workshop on Experiences with the Design and Implementation of Smart Objects*. ACM, 37–42.

[11] Sangyoung Park, Licong Zhang, and Samarjit Chakraborty. 2016. Design space exploration of drone infrastructure for large-scale delivery services. In *Proceedings of the 35th International Conference on Computer-Aided Design*. ACM, 72.

[12] Giuseppe Procaccianti, Patricia Lago, Antonio Vetro, Daniel Méndez Fernández, and Roel Wieringa. 2015. The green lab: Experimentation in software energy efficiency. In *Proceedings of the 37th International Conference on Software Engineering-Volume 2*. IEEE Press, 941–942.

[13] Kaufui Vincent Wong. 2015. Research and development of drones for peace - high power high energy supply required. *Journal of Energy Resources Technology* 137, 3 (2015), 034702.

[14] Dimitrios Zorbas, Tahiry Razafindralambo, Francesca Guerriero, et al. 2013. Energy efficient mobile target tracking using flying drones. *Procedia Computer Science* 19 (2013), 80–87.

Climate Change: Relationships to CO_2 Emission and Locations

Mandar Kadam
School of Applied Technology
Illinois Institute of Technology
Chicago, Illinois, USA 60616
mkadam1@hawk.iit.edu

Nisha Kanoo
School of Applied Technology
Illinois Institute of Technology
Chicago, Illinois, USA 60616
nkanoo@hawk.iit.edu

Yong Zheng
School of Applied Technology
Illinois Institute of Technology
Chicago, Illinois, USA 60616
yzheng66@iit.edu

ABSTRACT

The global climate change has been one of the serious problems in the 21st century. In this paper, we analyze the correlations or patterns associated with the global temperature data, carbon-dioxide emission and the location information based on the latitude or longitude. We do find some interesting patterns, especially the ones based on latitude or longitude information. The analytical results can be used to better understand the characteristics of climate change in different locations.

CCS CONCEPTS

• **Applied computing** → *Computers in other domains*;

KEYWORDS

climate change; longitude; latitude

1 INTRODUCTION

In the past decades, we have experienced serious problems in global warming. Schlesinger, et al. [1] claimed the correlation between CO_2 emissions and the changes in global temperature and precipitation. Simpson, et al. [2] additionally investigated the relationship between regions and temperature in Europe. In this paper, we are able to integer enough data to experimentally examine these correlations in order to reveal interesting patterns in the climate changes.

2 EXPERIMENTS AND FINDINGS

The first data[1] we use contains the temperature, latitude, longitude at city/state/country levels. The second one[2] captures the CO_2 emission associated with countries between 1990 and 2013. Both of them cover information associated with more than 200 countries.

2.1 Temperature Change v.s. CO_2 Emission

We build linear regression models to explore the impact by CO_2 emission on the temperature. More specifically, we focus on four countries: USA, India, China and United Kingdom. We find that the optimal linear models actually produce high prediction errors and are poor (i.e., average adjusted R square is around 0.42) to explain

[1]https://kaggle.com/berkeleyearth/climate-change-earth-surface-temperature-data
[2]http://edgar.jrc.ec.europa.eu/overview.php?v=CO2ts_pc1990-2013

the observations. It can tell that CO_2 emission may be one of the influential factors but other greenhouse gases, such as methane, nitrous oxide and water vapor, should be taken into account to better predict the climate changes.

2.2 Temperature Change v.s. Locations

Particularly, we are interested in the temperate change for specific countries that are located at similar latitude or longitude. Figure 1 presents the average temperature changes for Brazil, Indonesia and Somalia located at latitude 0.80N. Countries in similar latitude or longitude may present similar curves in temperature changes, but we believe water sources may play an important role. Coastal regions, such as Indonesia which is surrounded with the ocean, are showing inconsistent patterns with Brazil and Somalia. Climate change in Brazil and Somalia show similar curves but the degree of temperature changes is different.

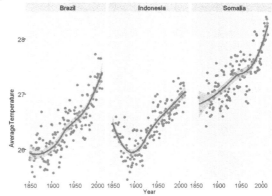

Figure 1: Average temperature of countries at latitude 0.80N

We further explore the coastal and continental regions in USA. The climate change is much more constant and stable in the coastal areas (such as California), while the continental parts (such as Iowa) present a rise in temperature. The coastal areas have more moderate temperatures because oceans may take longer time to heat or cool.

These observed patterns are useful to help us better understand the characteristics of climate changes in different regions. It also infers that the solutions for global warming could be generated according to the location characteristics, e.g., we may use different solutions to the coastal and continental areas.

REFERENCES

[1] Michael E Schlesinger and John FB Mitchell. 1987. Climate model simulations of the equilibrium climatic response to increased carbon dioxide. *Reviews of Geophysics* 25, 4 (1987), 760–798.
[2] Isla R Simpson, Tiffany A Shaw, and Richard Seager. 2014. A diagnosis of the seasonally and longitudinally varying midlatitude circulation response to global warming. *Journal of the Atmospheric Sciences* 71, 7 (2014), 2489–2515.

Internet of Things BLE Security

Thomas Chiu, David Calero Luis, Vinesh Jethva
School of Applied Technology
Illinois Institute of Technology
Wheaton, IL, 60189
tchiu2@hawk.iit.edu, dcaleroluis@hawk.iit.edu, vjethva@hawk.iit.edu

ABSTRACT

Bluetooth Low Energy device is increasing in popularity due to its lower energy consumption and reliable connectivity compared to the classic Bluetooth. Some of these BLE devices collects and transmits health care data like the heart rate as in a Fitbit smart band. This paper will demonstrate that Bluetooth Low Energy devices that relies on BLE security has weak communication security and how to solve that problem using a private-key encryption algorithm.

CCS CONCEPTS: • Security and privacy~Public key encryption; • Security and privacy~Security protocols

KEYWORDS: ACM; BLE

1 INTRODUCTION

Oxford Dictionary has the definition of "the Internet of Things" as the interconnection via the internet of computing devices embedded in everyday objects, enabling them to send and receive data. The IoT devices appear in various aspects of our daily life. As the number of devices that use this technology increases, security of the data exchanged among them is considered a major concern for the users of these devices.

In this paper, our focus will be placed on the Bluetooth Low Energy protocol. An emulated Heart Rate Monitor is built using the Intel Arduino 101. Together with the Heart Rate Monitor, a Bluetooth Low Energy (BLE) test environment Fig. 1 is set up to expose the vulnerability of the communication for the BLE device. In order to be able to retrieve the password used to encrypt the communication (if any), we need to capture BLE packets containing the messages exchanges during the generation of the new key.

2 KEY EXCHANGE PROTOCOL

One interesting thing about the key exchange protocols that already came with the Bluetooth Low Energy protocol is not well-known and they are a 3-stage process and are provided by

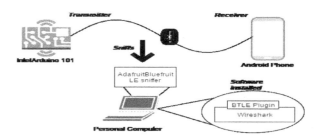

Figure 1: **Bluetooth Low Energy test environment**

the Link Layer encryption. The curious fact about these key exchange protocols is that none of them provide protection against a passive eavesdropper, so anyone that is able to listen the establishment of the connection would be able to obtain the private key used to encrypt the PDU of all BLE packets transmitted over that connection. They are as follows: 6-digit Pin, Just Works, and Out of Band (OOB).

3 PROPOSED SOLUTION

In order to prevent the security issue of the key exchange protocols already built-in BLE, we recommend exchanging the keys using the Diffie-Hellman algorithm, which has been tested and it is considered secure.

Once we have a secure key distribution algorithm, the next step is to use a secure encryption algorithm to encrypt the data being transmitted in the BLE packets. In this case, we have used AES in CCM mode.

4 CONCLUSION

We demonstrated that the security used by BLE is very weak as the wireless algorithms for the key distribution are susceptible to eavesdropping, and we have proposed a secure way to encrypt the communication that can be implemented in every IoT device. We have seen and demonstrate the vulnerabilities for the built-in protocols of Bluetooth Low Energy and how to exploit them.

With all this, we want to demonstrate that it's very easy and simple to implement good security in Bluetooth Low Energy communications, as it can be done with low computational resources and with a low consumption of energy. For all previous reasons, we think that manufacturer should focus more on security when relying in BLE, so that consumer data will be safe from any near attacker.

Author Index

www.ingramcontent.com/pod-product-compliance
Lightning Source LLC
LaVergne TN
LVHW060149070326
832902LV00018B/3016